Salt and sensuality. Walk the seashore. Enjoy your stay on a quiet island resort off the coast. With bocce courts and group swimming, it's the perfect respite for those of a certain age. But after dark, things really warm up.

Welcome to Moon Pools, the fake cover band created by Gregory von Portz and Ashley Rebecca King, most commonly found at your favorite, fictitious, mid-level-luxury resort. Inspired by their sold-out, standing-room-only shows, Moon Pools presents *Moon Pools: Kindness is Edgy*— a pool party book for their hippest and most sophisticated friends. Menthol-cool stylings and intellectual discourse abound, as the reader is treated to a literary interpretation of a show that's been recommended by the *New York Times*, the *Village Voice*, *Time Out New York* and fans around the globe.

"The quirky and brash hilarity of Portz's storytelling mixed with the comedic deadpan and piano technique of King make for a delightful evening out of escapism."
— **Examiner**

"This surreal mash-up of music and theatrics makes this *BACKLASH* worth listening to."
— **Time Out New York**

"...unpredictable cabaret style..."
— **Village Voice**

"...loud—way too loud."
— **Talkin' Broadway**

To
Elaine + Lee

With many warm
wishes for the
coming year

Geoff

4

MOON POOLS

Kindness is Edgy

The Collected Works of
Gregory von Portz and Ashley Rebecca King

Polynesian Moods Publishing House

New York

Tuscarora

North Versailles

Printed in the United States of America

First Edition

BOOKCOVER DESIGN BY Graham McCarty
INTERIOR ILLUSTRATIONS & LAYOUT DESIGNED
by
Ashley Rebecca King
www.portzandking.com

To our respective parents

*(whose names are purposefully
omitted due to foreseeable,
drawn-out, inter-family conflicts.)*

MOON POOLS

Kindness is Edgy

The Collected Works of
Gregory von Portz and Ashley Rebecca King

Ladies and gentlemen, my name is Gregory von Portz and my coauthor is the wild, talented and exotic Ashley Rebecca King.

A lot of people have called this book a lot of different things: an autobiography, a work of staggering beauty, a vanity project. But this book is really just us reaching out and checking in with you, our fans.

What is a "book" anyway? Just some paper bound together with some words on it? Something you put your glass on because you ran out of coasters? Digital flotsam and jetsam? Well, yes, but to me, a book is a dance—a fever-pitched tarantella for the eyes, soul and heart (if you have eyes, soul and heart).

Browsing through a bookstore today, you might feel overwhelmed. It's a labyrinthine journey leaving you unfulfilled. Why make reading more complicated and boring than it already is?

With this in mind, we kept the concept for this simple. *Moon Pools*—the book—is, merely, a tropical-lifestyle travel guide-cum-poetry, coffee table book you can take anywhere, as well as a musical-on-paper, with elements of graphic novels and Aristotelian drama. It's also a children's book.

Within these pages, you'll find some of our most beloved stories, photos, advice, art, and odd, abstract transcripts from past shows. Maybe some of it makes sense, maybe it doesn't. The important thing is—you bought it. I hope you can read it as quickly as it was written.

Welcome. Welcome to Moon Pools.

With love and kindness,

Gregory von Portz

&

Ashley Rebecca King

"Sometimes, late at night, I get really down. I feel a sadness from deep within me. My throat closes from the grief. Then, I realize that somewhere—on this great expanse of land, water and sky, beneath the blazing glory of the sun—someone just like you or me is having an unwanted pregnancy. And that makes me feel so much better. "

A piano sits onstage. There's a blonde woman bludgeoning the ivory keys and a man, center, strangling the neck of a mic. The blood-red curtains make the pair, the microphone and the piano look like shadows. They're cutouts, cartoons, paper dolls.

It's casual-slash-elegant attire in this "underground" club. Not many things can be considered "underground" in a tourist hellscape town like this. Oddly, the club is in a family resort hotel. The commercials on TV with the annoying bald man proclaim it's for "families who want the best time without spending a lot of dimes." But the Hotel del Mar, like all other hotels in the del Mar chain, turns out to be a rundown, flophouse of a place. While the name implies seafront, it's a long walk to any beach, and the safest

13

way to get there is on one of the hotel-owned surrey carts. Even then, you'll only get to the abandoned boardwalk or the newly-built hurricane wall.

The pool could be the only refuge from the unseasonably-tropic heat. You wish you were in the pool right now. But you can't be, since the owners installed a clear plexiglass floor over it. This very club hovers above the splashing, blue-green algal punch. The hollow water thud is unsettlingly loud beneath the audience of drunk parents, the hippest of the hip, sunburned wives widowed by gambling, and foreign tourists.

And then—there's you. You're sitting with a new friend you picked up as you walked along the abandoned boardwalk. You shared a surrey ride back to the hotel, and then a kiss. Your head is dizzy from the French 75s. You shift in the sagging velvet seats. The whole place smells like a hotel lobby: perfume, mixed with tannic wines and the moist aroma of cheap cheese plates. You find it amusing that the waitrons in this dump are wearing white gloves—beautiful, bleached, star-white gloves. White hands dancing above the filth-covered tables and candlelight like seagulls.

You've always thought of yourself as an inland seagull. At some point a storm blew you off course. Sometimes, your previous life seems like a dream. You're lost and bewildered by the birds who find it so easy to make their small nests and subsist on

14

worms. Bullfinches, grosbeaks, finches, woodpeckers, even cardinals and the blue jays are content with their piney, treetop enclaves. These birds nest in bushes, some nest on the ground. Talk about not living up to expectations. Birds should soar! Your inland kin sing all of the time: sweet songs of spring, sweet songs of winter, sweet songs of fall. You don't want sweet, you want salty—you crave the ocean. You long for the summer. That's what brought you to this coastal town.

Glasses clink, there's the hum of applause breaking; the lights go up on a small stage. Smoke curls around the slow-moving ceiling fan. It shatters quietly like a wave and spreads from side to side. Its ghostly fumes hang in the air; its particulate matter dances with the small flecks of dust through the luminescent discharge of the spotlight. There's a giant, wooden crescent-moon hanging above the stage. In the haze, it looks surreal and ominous.

You're nervous. You've read about Moon Pools. Friends told you you should come, but reminded you to drink beforehand and bring money for merchandise. While you've enjoyed the show so far, you have a sinking feeling that you'll be called on stage. Audience participation: your biggest nightmare. The last time you were on stage, you were humiliated. The duo is in the middle of a medley. You're laughing. The show is almost over. You're safe. You take a drag of a cigarette.

Greg and Ashley are looking at you now. You feel someone pulling you up by the hand toward the stage. All eyes on you— everyone is laughing.

It's time you stopped eating worms.

Portz & King - Backstage

Recipe for Hotel del Mar's French 75

1 lemon
4 tablespoons gin
1 oz fresh lemon juice
1 tablespoon (1/2 ounce) simple syrup
1 cup ice cubes
1/4 cup (2 ounces) dry sparkling wine, such as brut Champagne, chilled

BACKLASH

Performed by Portz & King

Partial monologue transcribed from
unauthorized audio recording

July 4th, New York City

*The line for the show is long. Fans and first
timers have been chanting for Portz and
King to open the doors to the theater. The
room smells of hay. Indeed, there's hay
strewn about the stage, probably a bale's
worth. Long ropes of paper chain festoon
the theater. The microphone stands are
wrapped in bistro lights.*

GREGORY VON PORTZ enters theater;
ASHLEY REBECCA KING sits at piano
(Improvisational scatting)

*The music is urban mixed with Southern
gothic hymns.*

GREGORY VON PORTZ:
Life can be any way you want it.
It can be like the best movie you've ever seen.
It can be like a beautiful novel.
Or, it can be like a show in a shitty, poorly
decorated theater with a basketball hoop in
the corner.

Ladies and gentlemen, I'm Gregory von Portz and this is the beautiful and exotic Ashley Rebecca King.

(Transcriber's note: much cheering)

Now, we've made a lot of mistakes in our life, but you can't let the past get you down. You know what you gotta do when the past gets you down? You gotta...

Music cue: "Turn the Beat Around"

BACKLASH: the stage

Reflections on a Leaf
Excerpt from Ashley's Diary
Cinco de Mayo

I keep a leaf in my drawer
It's not green anymore
But I keep it anyway
It represents life,
Though it's decayed.

I keep a leaf
in my drawer.

Collecting is in your blood, it drips through your veins like syrup from a sturdy maple in the spring. Your father was a collector, your grandfather was a collector and here you are—a collector.

Dad collected stamps. To this day, you can't lick an envelope without wanting to vomit. Your Saturdays were spent in the basement counting, licking and sticking stamps in a book. Grandpa collected pornography—a hobby he also kept to the basement. He never showed it to you; you found it during a game of hide and seek. You weren't disgusted, but curious about the coiled bodies and all of the hair. Why would someone need five-hundred explicit magazines? What makes somebody compelled to hoard?

You found the answer. Not in titty mags, but your need to collect is as strong as your father's and your grandfather's. To call it a *need* is offensive to what it really is—collecting is a way of existence. It's what keeps you off the precipice, soothes you and makes you whole.

You collect something different. You collect words, in your head and on paper. All of the things that rush through people's' minds you remember, so you record them. The first time this happened was in second grade. It was the spring play and you remembered everything they said on stage, went home and wrote everything down in a composition book.

That's what you do with Moon Pools. You've seen almost all of their shows, several hundred at this point. You remember everything: the location, the set list, the costumes—always black—and the number of people in the audience. You've also collected many additional items from the Moon Pools cannon. You've transcribed, clipped, researched, compiled, binded, copied, collated, pasted and arranged everything you could get your hands on. You draw for them. They may never see it. You want them to see it.

<u>This</u> is your collection.

Balcony of a rented apartment,
waiting for a Moon Pools show
Barcelona, Spain

A FIST FULL OF LOVE - song list
A Comedy Created by Greg Portz and Ashley King

Clocks

Opening
- The Squirrel Shuffle - original
- Nine to Five
- Life in a Northern Town
- Since You've Been Gone

Mama was a Vagabond - original

Joyful Joyful/ Bohemian Rhapsody

The King Must Die

Free Your Mind

The Entertainer

7166

Lemon Laundromat

PERFORMER KING & PORTZ	PERFORMER KING / PORTZ
PAID COVER 13 × 8 =	PAID COVER 12 × 8 = 96 -
MAC	MAC
RETURN DEPOSIT	RETURN DEPOSIT
LESS TECH	LESS TECH
LESS EXTRA COMP	LESS EXTRA COMP 60 -
LESS PICK UP CHECK	LESS PICK UP CHECK
LESS MISC.	LESS MISC. 13 01
AMOUNT PAID	AMOUNT PAID 22.99
PAID COVERS	PAID COVERS
MAC	MAC 12
COMPS ALLOWED	COMPS ALLOWED
EXTRA COMPS	EXTRA COMPS 1
PRESS COMPS	PRESS COMPS
PROF COMPS/HOUSE CO	PROF COMPS/HOUSE COMPS
AUDEINT EXTRA	AUDEINT EXTRA
COVER/MISC.	COVER/MISC.
TOTAL GUESTS	TOTAL GUESTS 16
(DAVI)	(DAVI)
BY:	BY: 09/05/06 DATE

Items (clockwise from left corner)
#14, 308, 131 & 132

24

Individual item descriptions:

Note: All Items Salvaged from Upper East Side apartment March 27th

#14: *A Fist Full of Love* set list

"A Comedy Created by Greg Portz and Ashley King"

"Clocks"

Opening:

- "The Squirrel Shuffle" - original
- "Nine to Five"
- "Life in a Northern Town"
- "Since You've Been Gone"

"Mama Was a Vagabond" - original
"Joyful, Joyful"/"Bohemian Rhapsody"
"The King Must Die"
"Free Your Mind"
"The Entertainer"

#308: Receipt from
Lemon Laundromat for Greg Portz
14 lbs
"No Downy"
"No Bleach"
"Only my soap, please"

#131 & 132: Show Receipts
from unidentified Portz & King show
signed by "David"

Moon Pools: Trade Winds

Travelogue, Printed from Memory
February 28th

A terrible Lithuanian pimp named
Dominicus was holding us, by our feet, over
the ledge of a rehearsal studio building in
New York City. Ashley was screaming,
begging and pleading for our lives. The deal
for our musical *Mama, Don't Preach* had just
gone terrible awry. This was just a week ago.

"How did we get here?" I thought to myself.

Well, just a week prior, we were in a terrible
shootout in a small cafe in Tangier. Blood
was running down the walls, the piano was
broken, the audience had scattered leaving
their unfinished drinks at the table. Ashley
was screaming, begging and pleading for our
lives.

"How did we get here?" I said aloud.

Well, a year prior to the day of the attack in
the small cafe, and a year and two weeks
from the day of us being held by our feet over
the side of a building, I found Ashley in an
alley in Prague singing "Fooled Around and
Fell in Love" for money. I wasn't in a much
better state at the time...but my song
selection was. I was singing our old
European hit—a cover of Dave Brubeck's
"Take Five."

Oh, Ashley, remember? Remember the good ole' days?

Some of you may or may not know, but Ashley and I haven't performed in the States together for over two years!

"How did we get here, then?" you may be asking yourselves.

Well, almost two years ago to this very date, we were performing *Moon Pools: So Emotional*. It was a tribute to the death of Whitney Houston. You see, at the time we were just doing Moon Pools for fun—a lark—as a way to express ourselves while we worked on our big jukebox musical called *Mama, Don't Preach*: a story about love, racism and climate change.

In the audience for that performance was a writer for a small, German newspaper, *Der Spiegel*. He wrote us up and said what others had said before: Moon Pools is "too loud", "akin to rape" and "cruel and unusual."

The Germans loved us! And after our cover of "Take Five" by Dave Brubeck hit the airwaves we booked a giant tour of Europe. Surely, if they liked us, they'd love *Mama, Don't Preach*.

Then, something strange started to happen—the Europeans took to Ashley a little more than me. You see, at this time, Ashley was pretending to be a man. Why, behind my back, Ashley recorded a version of "Fooled Around and Fell in Love" as her male stage persona Adam Rebecca King. I was devastated, especially after her single was on the Japanese Hit Parade. *Mama, Don't Preach* would never see the light of day.

I went to France and rented a small flat in the Loire Valley. I cried nightly. I talked to the mice in my apartment, they were my only friends. I took to smoking a marijuana cigarette once a day and taking Valium (to take the edge of the weed off). Thus began my hallucinations. I'd never see my work onstage. I was drinking heavily. And talking to those goddamned mice: "How are you today, Skippy?" "What's up, Mimsy?" All of my mice were WASPy New Englanders in my head. They were the only living things who would listen to me sing. I loved those mice, until one of them chewed through my box of spicy Cheez-Its. I thought it would be better to kill them all in one fell swoop. I hooked the exhaust pipe from a truck through my window, let it run and left. My poor landlady. I hear her last words were, "Gregory von Portz." What a lovely gesture. I could have just rested on that, but I had a career to revive.

At one point, there was the whole kidnapping ordeal and I ended up homeless in Belgrub. Now, Belgrub is often referred to as "the Paris of Eastern Europe." Anytime you call anywhere "the Paris of" something, you know you're in trouble.

Valderi, valdera. There was I, on the streets— a hobo without a home—though I still had the voice of an angel, albeit a down-on-his-luck one. In every town square, open-air restaurant and children's museum you'd hear me singing "Take Five" by Dave Brubeck.

And then, in an alley, I ran into Ashley, also singing for money.

How did she get here?

Ashley was living in Hong Kong where her music career tanked after she expressed anti-Chinese government sentiment. She became a subsistence farmer, but her crop of choice was Concord grapes, which don't grow in semi-tropical climates, and only are in season for, like, two weeks in September. And everyone forgets to buy them and is all, like: "Well I guess I'll have to remember them next year, 'cause they taste like grape. No, seriously, like real grape. Well, candy grape. Grape flavor, they're the real grape flavor. They're so good."

Ms. King felt bad about *Mama, Don't Preach* never getting off of the ground. And with her firm body, big eyes and lack of self-respect she became a prostitute to save money and eventually produce the show. She was, as in her music career, performing her sex work as a man. Her pimp was a Lithuanian bruiser named Dominicus.

Ashley was having a good time and making tons of cash under the *nom de sexe:* Adam. One day, Dominicus saw "Adam" coming out of Curves—a gym for women. He flew off the handle and started shooting at her. Ashley ran as fast as she could from Hong Kong, through Siberia, until she ended up singing on the streets.

There we were. Moon Pools. Bygones became bygones.

We sang "Take Five" by Dave Brubeck together in perfect-ish harmony. But, our happiness was cut short when Dominicus appeared out of nowhere again. Ashley and I hopped on a surrey cart and pushed through Eastern Europe, into Western Europe, over the Alps to the piedmont, to France, over the Pyrenees, through Spain until we arrived in Tangier, Morocco.

Inspired by the influences of the wild and exotic city, we decided to work on *Mama, Don't Preach*: a musical that takes place in

New York City after a ten-year drought. Ashley and I were in hiding at this time, too, so we performed under the name Poon Mools, you know, to throw Dominicus off of our tail. I bought a gun just to be safe, because there is nothing safer than a gun.

One lovely evening, we were performing:

> "Ladies and gentlemen, welcome to Poon Mools. We'd like to do a little tune that has always brought us luck. It's a little ditty by the name of "Take Five" by David Brube..."

A gunshot fired. Dominicus had found us.

I took my gun and shot several times. Ashley, as she is trained to do, set the piano on fire and pushed it into the audience. There was complete chaos as gunfire ripped through the cafe. After the melee, blood dripped from the walls. Poon Mools...no, Moon Pools was victorious.

All of a sudden, out of nowhere, without warning Dominicus pulled himself up from under the rubble and started to chase us. Ashley was screaming, begging, pleading for our lives. I screamed, "I'm pregnant!" Dominicus got confused and we ran and got the nearest surrey cart. We took that surrey to a car which we drove to the Atlantic Ocean, then sealed up the top and converted into a submarine. Dominicus was right behind us the whole time, shooting up a storm. Bullets were constantly missing us.

Once we got to the United States, we immediately got on a train and Dominicus followed on horseback. All through the contiguous U.S. and then Hawaii, that train flew. We finally docked the train in New York City. We were safe. No more Dominicus to harm us. I wondered what happened to him.

Valderi, valdera—we got a big backers' audition for *Mama, Don't Preach*. The potential producer heard about Moon Pools and wanted to take us on. His name was Mominicus from Mithuania. We were so excited.

Ashley and I walked into the rehearsal studio, ready to regale this producer with a story about Christa and droughts. We opened the big, white doors and—there was Dominicus.

And that, ladies and gentlemen, is how we ended up dangling over the side of the building.

SET LIST - Moon Pools: Trade Winds
February 28th, NYC
(special requests underlined}

Ashley(pre-show)
- "Moon River"
- "Over the Rainbow"
- "On the Sunny Side of the Street"
- "Beautiful" (Bossa Nova)
- "You've Got a Friend in Me"
- "Will You Still Love Me Tomorrow"
- "Love" (samba)
- "Take Me Back to Manhattan"
- "Blue Moon"

INTRODUCE GREG/ OPENING
- "I Feel Love"/ "Groove is in the Heart"

BLUE BIRDS MONOLOGUE
- "You Only Live Twice"/"Fly Me to the Moon"

TRAVELOGUE (Subject to Change)
- "Fooled Around and Fell in Love"
- "Genie in a Bottle" (Spanish)
- "OH! You Pretty Things"
- "Head, Shoulders, Knees and Toes"
- "Radio GaGa"
- "Don't Dream It's Over"
- "3:45 No Sleep"
- "This Must Be the Place"

TEACH "MAN IN THE MIRROR"
"HOW DEEP IS YOUR LOVE"/"LOVE ON TOP"
CRAFT/ INTERVIEW
- "I'm Gonna Make you Love me" (Bathroom Break)
- "Gotta Be" / "Proud"
MEDITATION - "Imagine"

WORLD PREMIERE:
MAMA DON'T PREACH (A Jukebox Musical)
- see separate set list
(performed using audience "volunteers")
FINALE
-"MAN IN THE MIRROR" sing-along
-"I TRY"
"CLOSING TIME"

Item #318: set list

33

Message in a Wine Bottle I

Dear Editor,

I don't know how you'll be reading this, what devices you'll be using to glaze over the text. Perhaps, by the time we get out of here, you'll be able to read in the air—the words will just pop up. Or maybe reading won't be something humans do anymore. Reading will go the way of talking and love. I hope, in whatever media you are reading this, you paid for it. I also hope that we're getting a cut of that, that we didn't sign some crooked deal with a deadbeat publisher. Worse yet, I hope it's not self-published. If any of these things come true, don't tell me. I won't be able to take it. After being a castaway like this, I don't think I can take too much more.

I'm writing this from a desert island. Every morning, I wake up, write, then put the manuscript into an empty bottle and send it to you, our editor, a music teacher in North Versailles, Pennsylvania. There are no empty bottles on this island. Thus, I'm forced to drink a bottle of wine every morning just to create a vessel to send off my work. (I found several cases of wine in a cave.)

Ashley's off foraging most of the day. What an uninspiring task. Yesterday, she brought back an off-brand roasted chicken. I threw it into the ocean. I said if the locals can't roast it like they do it in New York City, I don't even want it.

The air-conditioner in my room sometimes makes a guitar-sounding noise at night, and I pray that someday we'll return safely to our rental apartments.

I thought we escaped the worst of ship life, mainly getting a stomach virus.

The shipwreck was less traumatic than a plane crash, but more awful than a fender-bender. The water filled the ship during one of our sets. The sound of dolphins was so loud, we had to turn the sound up; they must have been breeding.

We were in the middle of our ode to Bossa Nova called Bossa N(ode)va as the water rose and people screamed. I have waking nightmares of the screams. Nevertheless, I was very disappointed with the Tex-mex buffet on that cruise ship; I'm glad it sank.

I hope we leave this island and find these missives, sent periodically via bottle and ocean, have made it into some bound form.

Kindness Is Edgy,

Gregory von Portz

"The 4 O'Clock Song"

Portz & King, 2004

I have no noble passion
I care only for myself
If charity's in fashion
Then my style needs help
I've no time for the helpless
No time for the needy
I've tried to be selfless
But luxuries impede me

The needs of others
Are not my needs
So why leave my pockets
To bleed
And the wants of others
Frankly aren't mine
I'm apathy's paradigm

The women on corners
Passing out brochures,
Children
and the Falun Gong, too
These are all people
I choose to ignore
Don't judge me
You do it, too.

My existential habit
Brings me to drink
But I drink only
The finest wine
It's not my fault

36

I'm on a roll
And not the government's dole
And all of my money is mine

And the needs of others
Are not my needs
Is that greed?
No, it isn't indeed
The wants of others
Simply aren't mine
I'm apathy's paradigm

Time Signature Change: 9/8

Now I'm not a loaner
Not one for alms-giving
But it's four in the morning
And I look out my window
I see all the people
I think I might help them...

But then I don't care

La La La
La La La (*repeat and fade*)

presents

A FIST FULL OF LOVE

With Ashley King and Greg Portz

Tuesday September 5
And
Thursday September 7
9:15 PM
Danny's Skylight Room

Item #42: (left) Performer check from
Danny's Grand Sea Palace in NYC
Item #56: (right) Program from *A Fist Full of Love*

IN A POLYNESIAN MOOD

PRE-SHOW

- Greg asleep on stage

OPENING

- "Tonight, Tonight"
- Monologue:
    "I'm on an island…"
- "Tonight, Tonight"/
    "Don't Stop Me Now" Medley

THE TAKE-AWAY TOUR

- "C'mon to my House"
- "MacArthur's Park"
- "Gimme a Pigfoot"

MIDDLE

POCONOS

- "River Deep, Mountain High"

NEPAL/ FUNERAL

- "Ah, a Little Death"

BRANSON

- "How Far We've Come"

END

- Monologue – NYC/ Audition
- "Manhattan Island Serenade"
- Finale (Medley)

Item # 95: Set List

You're in Chinatown. The streets gleam with spit and the blood of animals. You'd be able to get home easily in any other Chinatown, but this particular one is in Shanghai. Maybe there is no Chinatown in a Chinese town. Hmmm, you think to yourself. No, there wouldn't be a Chinatown in a town in China. Ok, let's just say you are in Shanghai in China.

The winter moon is hanging low. The cold, jade wind pushes against your back. You seek shelter in a cafe. The walls are red and everyone looks suspicious. What did you get yourself into?

"Happy New Year," someone whispers into your ear. They hand you a pipe. You inhale deeply. There are only a few moments from that night you'll remember: a rickshaw ride through the Bund with a group of French millionaires, singing Gershwin at the top of your lungs on Nanjing Road as the fireworks light up the night sky, seeing Moon Pools in an underground club and making love at dawn in the Yuyuan Garden. It's the year of the Boar. When you wake up in your hotel, it'll be as if the whole thing never happened—but it did.

You awake and search frantically for a bootleg copy of the Moon Pools show you saw last night. You've been following Moon Pools around ever since you first saw them. You thought they were going to pull you onstage, but it was a trick. Gregory von Portz grabbed your hand and then let go. Let go of you. You won't let go of them, you can't. The show you are looking for is called *In a Polynesian Mood*. It's not the first show they did together, but it's the best according to fans.

You've researched their lives heavily. They began their career in a now defunct Thai restaurant called Danny's Skylight Cabaret Room. Blossom Dearie would go on before them and sit in the Thai restaurant and sign autographs. Greg and Ashley had no clue who she was. They laughed at her.

You're laughing at yourself now, since you don't have enough money for a cab and can only afford...the surrey cart that is pulling up alongside the road.

Puddles and people are your main takeaway from Shanghai that rainy day. The fish market is redolent with smells that a fish market would have. Frantic searching ensues on your part.

Finally, amid the squid ink and octopus rectums you see it scrawled in Ashley's handwriting: *In a Polynesian Mood*. It's the only copy ever made.

A Fish Market in Shanghai

In a Polynesian Mood

A poem by Gregory von Portz

I'm on an island.
The sound of the ocean is deafening;
I can hear it on all sides

I'm on an island.
A land with no trees,
no beaches—
just jagged rocks dropping into the abyss.

Birds fly overhead, but
never land.

The same birds are
carved into stone.
Carved by someone who
lived so long ago, that to
think about the time
would only remind you of
your own mortality.

Green.
Everywhere.
How empty it seems
with only my dreams.

I look at the stone carving of the bird.
Its eyes light up.

Instead of being startled,
I'm relieved.

There's some form of life here.
Even if it's spirits of the ancients.
Even if it is just my imagination.

I'm thirsty.
I look for water
I turn all the way around—

Nothing.

My gaze returns to the stone bird.
It's just stone.
I lay down on the grass to rest my head.
I assume there are no predators,
since there's no prey.

A loud caw—almost a crow sound—wakes me
"Trial and error," a voice says.
Not in English.
Not in any language I've heard;
I can understand it though.

I look at the stone statue of the bird again.
I'm certain its familiarity will ease my fear.

The stone has turned into a real bird.
It's walking toward me.
Its gait is awkward, like a child moving a
puppet.

Closer – Closer - Closer

We're eye-to-eye
"Go to the water." it says, then flies away.

I run toward the water.
Memories, photos and words flood into my
mind.

I see them:

The monoliths.

Large heads carved into stone,
Looking onto the ocean
Forever staring at a world
which they'll never see
and their builders had no hope—or maybe
just no interest—of seeing.

It was snowing inside the nightclub the same as it was outside when Beverly Allison stepped through the curtained doorway, but she did not mind. She shimmied out of her faux-fur coat and tossed it into the corner, abandoned forever. It didn't matter. It wasn't hers. Neither was the name. She'd borrowed it from the cover of a children's book she'd passed by in the darkened window of Shakespeare and Co. on the journey across town. Tonight she was a Phoenix. Tonight she was reborn.

Almost immediately, she was approached by a male bystander offering her a drink and a dance, but she dismissed him with a coo. She wanted to savor the moment without a beverage in hand. She weaved her way around the jagged edge of the dance floor, passing beautiful triplets and quartets of revelers embracing the electronic throb of sound. She approached the bar, thick with conspirators. She lingered there for awhile watching their primitive interactions. No one spoke to her. She was beginning to regret turning down the initial offer. Then the man next to her ended his drink request with "And whatever the lady wants" and her confidence returned. She ordered something "Pink. With vodka." In thanks, she nodded her head at her benefactor, but refused to engage in conversation.

She carried her drink to the next level, passing two identical women burning each other with cigarette butts on a loveseat. It was so surreal she didn't think to stop them. She floated around the circumference of the terrace, passing through out-stretched limbs like a ghost. She tried hard to look bored.

Two songs later, she found a seat on a tattered couch next to a man and a woman arguing quietly. The snow had stopped by then, replaced by a rainbow that doused the crowd below, transforming those assembled into trembling jelly beans. A sapphire beam fell on her as well, as she leaned into the aged cushions, tucking her tiny feet beneath her. She closed her eyes, took a sip from her cup, and wondered how long she could stay.

Something "Pink. With Vodka"

Billy the Bunny: A children's tale

by Gregory von Portz

Copied from *Dogs Don't Love, They Die*
an unpublished collection of
children's tales and games

Billy was a bunny.
A cute bunny.
Billy the bunny hopped a lot.
He ate a lot too.
He hopped and ate and hopped some more.
He played in the fields and laid in the warm
sun on sunny days.

Billy's feet were tiny.
Billy wasn't the brightest bunny nor the most
capable bunny.
He hopped a lot, but couldn't read. Not
because bunnies can't read—they can—but
because Billy's mother drank while Billy was
in the womb. She also smoked marijuana and
fornicated while she was pregnant.
All of this made Billy woefully reduced in any
cerebral capacity.

Billy was a happy bunny.
Billy was a little bunny
Billy the bunny hopped a lot.
He yelled a lot too.

He hopped and ate and yelled and sometimes acted out violently in school.

He also did not have the social inhibitors that most bunnies have.
During one of his field hops he went completely manic and hopped from the safety of the field—into the world of humans!

He was racing, destination unknown.
He passed migrant workers waiting to be picked up for work.
He wasn't hopping anymore. Billy was flying—like a bird!

Over fences! Over tables!
Over cars!
Over houses!
And directly into a large swimming pool.

Bunnies can't swim.

A very thin, fit man by the name of Greg von Portz woke up one morning and took the aqua-blue pool skimmer, pulled Billy's dead body from the still water and threw the corpse into the neighbor's yard.

BACKLASH

Performed by Portz & King

Partial monologue transcribed from
unauthorized audio recording

July 4th, New York City

*After a thunderous applause break, Gregory
begins his monologue: a story of how he and
Ashley started out.*

GREGORY VON PORTZ:
Wow! What an opening. My good and lovely
friends—what a gorgeous night. Who would
think, on a night like this, we'd be thinking of
sad things? Tonight, ladies and gentlemen,
I'm thinking about loss. Maybe you lost
something important: a spouse, a friend,
your wallet.
But the kind of loss I'm thinking about is that
loss that hits you hard and deep.

Music cue Ashley only
"County Fair Theme"/ "Farm House"

Come back, come back with me to the county
fair. Close your eyes. Feel the hay beneath
your feet. Taste the cotton candy. Open your
nostrils and smell the animal manure...
OPEN YOUR EYES!! (Greg gags.) I can
taste it in my mouth.

Ashley and I met in preschool when I hit Ashley with a train set. She bled a lot, but c'est la vie. We started performing together in first grade. A few months later, we were asked to perform at the County Fair. I mean, we'd been waiting a lifetime to perform at the County Fair. We didn't take it lightly and practiced—for days.

Close your eyes. Imagine us on the stage, a summerstage, a talent contest portion of the fair: two little twelve-year-old kids in suits. Open your eyes.

Music cue: Greg and Ashley sing "Love Lift Us Up (Where We Belong)"

We wait backstage for our results and receive a 9.8 out of 10. Oh my god! We were going to win the blue ribbon.

CLOSE YOUR EYES AGAIN!

**Music cue Ashley only:
"Woman of the Ghetto"**

Picture a little girl, the next act: a mousy looking specimen, a little obese, with red, white and blue braces—it's Kay Hollywood, our nemesis in all things, but mostly music. She plays the flute. Her mother is a piano teacher. They're trash. You know, the kind of people who have wood paneling on their walls, and those 70s-style wall clocks made out of shellacked tree stumps. These were the type of suburban monsters who have magazines in their bathroom.

Open your eyes.

Music cue: "Love Lift Us Up (Where We Belong)" *for flute*

Kay waits confidently in her corner for the judge's decision: 9.81. Kay Hollywood wins the blue ribbon. We get the red ribbon. The red ribbon—second place.
It was humiliating. We don't like being humiliated.

The Old County Fairgrounds - no longer in use

"Mama Was a Vagabond"

Portz & King, 2004

Mama was a vagabond
And she liked to roam the land
Selling cocaine and moonshine
Out of the back of grandma's van
When she hit the town
She liked to sleep around
Mama was a vagabond

Daddy was a dirty drunk
And he liked to hit my dog
Spent all my mother's drug money buyin'
Guns from a catalogue
He liked to fight
In bars at night
Daddy was dirty drunk

Do the Vagabond
Do the Drunk
Do the Vagabond
Do the Drunk

Move your feet

Feel the funk

Everybody do the Drunk

Now I'm a drunken bum

And I sleep outside all day

Don't buy no drugs or sell no coke

But I manage to make my pay

'Cause everyday

On my birthday

I do the Vagabond on their graves

(For money)

V-A-G-A-B-O-N-D

Do the Vagabond

Do the Drunk

Move your feet

Feel the funk

Everybody do the Drunk

As the old saying goes, "Youth is wasted on the poor."

"Mommy! Mommy!"

"I'm stuck up here! Help me."

Your cries go unanswered. You're ten years old and you're stuck in the catalpa tree in your front yard for days. The sun dances as you watch it dip past the horizon three times.

"Mom! I'm hungry."

You can smell your mother making breakfast for your siblings as you sit in the tree. They're eating cooked eggs; you're eating raw robin eggs. Raw—like your emotions—like your feelings for your family. This is the family that left you up in that tree. This is the family that took your records away and burned them while you watched. This is the family that keeps magazines in their bathroom. Yes, magazines in a bathroom. They have all kinds of magazines. You've gone through all of them with disgust. Mostly they're out-of-date, some by eight years. The paper is wrinkled and warped from the humidity. Why didn't anyone ever clean them up?

A kindly neighbor retrieves you from the tree. At her house, she starts to play records for you. You fall in love with music. She tells you that when she dies, you'll get her records.

The next week, the brakes on her car were cut by an unknown person and she drove off of a cliff. She held true to her promise.

Excerpt from an untitled police procedural treatment

by Gregory von Portz
copied from page 27

Yo, yo, yo.
I'm rockin the boat.
Ya' better had sit down,
'Cause that ain't all she wrote.
Mess with me—I'll cut your throat
With a broken bottle
Then I'll steal your coat.
And you won't be singing note-for-note.

Now tru' dat, dat.
My pockets gettin' fat, fat.

I'm the bomb, and I don't take that lightly.
I makes more money than Keira Knightley.
If you think I'm hot
and you drunk,
then I might be.

I'm not one of those ho's who believes in
karma.
If you mess with me,
Then you mess with drama,
If I'm mad, then I know
I'm cuttin' somebody's mama.
And what?

The Most Beautiful Cat in the World

Zuko

Zuko is a Cat
Who is just a little fat
He covets your attention
But won't sit upon your lap
If you give him crunchy snacks & treats
He'll visit you for days
But if you call him "Precious"
He'll ignore you
And turn his head
Get on something he's not supposed to
Eat one of your birds
Build a secret train in your basement
Steal your credit card
Make a number of unauthorized
(And frankly embarrassing) purchases
Then leave you bankrupt
Or incarcerated
But he is the most beautiful cat in the world.

Message in a Wine Bottle II

Dear Editor,

I wanted a New World white wine in a chilled glass. It's summer, I thought. It's always summer here on the island. Even in the darkest of winters, I'd never wished the sun to be so hot. Ashley and I tried to fashion a time telling device out of an old watch. We ripped the thing apart and just ended up with some springs and gears and watch hands. At least the batteries are still good. We'll use those to shock fish to death.

What a pity that there aren't more things to eat on an island other than fish and off-brand rotisserie chickens. I'm still fuming at Ashley for putting that slop in front of me.

Once, I saw a TV show about an island where pigs come up to your boat to greet you. It made me happy. Pigs are my favorite non-dog animal. Ashley and I had a pig once; his name was Goggles and he died in a flood.

There's no New World white wine here. Old World whites only. Desert islands are the pits.

Hoping these letters are getting to you, dearest editor! I think they'll make for a great book.

Note: Perhaps Old World Whites is a good name for the book?

Kindness is Edgy,
Gregory von Portz

Goggles

Ashley's Recipe for Roasted Pork Shoulder

Ingredients:

Pork shoulder (any size, sometimes called a "picnic pork")

Salt

Pepper

Instructions:

Preheat oven to 200 degrees. Cover a baking sheet with aluminum foil. Place roasting rack on covered baking sheet. Liberally season pork shoulder with salt and pepper. Make sure to get some under the skin and in the crevices.

Roast skin side up until done, approximately 1 hour per pound. Once pork is fully cooked, crank the oven up to 500 degrees and roast 5 - 10 min per side, rotating the pork to crisp the skin.

Note: Please check internal temperature with a meat thermometer to determine doneness. Undercooked pork has strange effects on people.

Enjoy with rolls made from tapioca flour.

This dry climate isn't good for your skin. Are you getting sick, or is your throat just scratching from the arid air? It doesn't matter. Tonight you'll be seeing your favorite cover band, Moon Pools.

The drive through the desert was awe inspiring. Smooth, undulating shapes massaged your eyes. Hot reds and warm sepia colors surrounded you. The landscape's curves and ripples made the muscles in you back relax. Not a straight line in sight—except for the gas needle in your 1987 Chrysler LeBaron convertible, which is now dangerously low. Good thing there's a gas station up the road. Good thing you circled it on the map. The map was out-of-date (it came with the car), but gas stations don't move; they can't. What would happen to the gas tanks in the ground? Wouldn't it be a bigger undertaking to move all of those things? Wouldn't it be bad for the environment? What would happen to the wildlife? Do the tanks and pipes get reused? Stop thinking about anything other than Moon Pools.

Panic. There's the gas station—the closed gas station. **Stupid**. **Stupid**. You bang your head off the steering wheel in abject disgust for your ignorance. **Idiot**. It's really getting hot now. You're going to miss Moon Pools at the Hotel del Desierto. This trip of yours cost you your job.

You wish you were back seeing them for the first time, when the plexiglass floor cracked and the whole stage collapsed into the pool. You were almost on stage with them; Greg pulled you up there, then let you go. They made you feel alive. It was a dirty trick. They weren't really going to pull you up there.

Then, *crack*—yelling and a giant splash. You fell. The whole audience fell in, too. As you were bobbing up and down, you saw Gregory von Portz and Ashley Rebecca King floating off on top of a baby grand piano. You fell for Moon Pools—literally.

You're so hot now though. You get out of the car to search for water. You hear wheels squeaking slowly. Down the road is a man pushing a surrey cart with Hotel del Desierto written on the side. Without saying a word, you get in.

Day turns to night. The silent man pushes you through the desert. The lineless forms look like towering monsters. In the distance, you see the hotel. You hear the amps project Gregory von Portz singing, "Welcome to Moon Pools!" Your heart lights up. You hold a piece of paper to your chest,

an advertisement for this show you found in
your local paper.

You can't wait to see them again.

Maybe you'll even get on stage this time.

"Happiness hurts like that..."

Item # 27: drink umbrella
from first Moon Pools performance

Opening Monologue from
First *Moon Pools*

Transcribed from memory (musical cues omitted)
September 14th, Hotel del Mar

Ladies and gentlemen, we were doing a gig in Ocean City, NJ. This town—as everyone should know—is a dry town. That means: no alcohol at all, never, ever, never. Unfortunately, we had a three-week engagement at the Hotel del Mar, Ocean City.

For most cover bands, this gig would have been a blessing. But for us, it was a curse. Because Ashley has a *penchant*, which is French for "crippling addiction," for high-alcohol content beverages. But there wasn't a single beer to be served in Ocean City. Was there, Ashley? So, to make her feel better, and to cure her shakes, we do what we always do and we made some bathtub gin.

The recipe is as follows:
Just a little bit of *this*.
And a little bit of *that*.
You mix it all together and then—the hotel exploded.

But what was just so nice about the experience, and so very touching, was that *we* were the only survivors. It was a "feel good" moment...

Valderi, valdera. We had to go away to the next town over where we made a little beach shack out of driftwood. The wood just happened to have *drifted* from the construction site of an adjacent million-dollar home. There we were, in the shack, having a great time. Whoopsin' it up with the locals and partying, just living a beachy life.

There was a rumor about us floating around. Everyone kept saying that we attacked an elderly couple and robbed them for three-hundred dollars—which is ludicrous. I wouldn't attack anyone for less than a thousand dollars. I'm all about kindness.

It was a warm summer day. The sun was shining and the waves were crashing. Then, out of nowhere, a group of twenty police officers surrounded our little beach retreat. I didn't know what to do, so I spit some water at them.

Now, the papers said I shot at the officers with a semi-automatic weapon, which is also inaccurate, because I only like things that are automatic. Ashley was putting her jewelry in bread and swallowing it, just in case we were put in prison. (We've been there before and know that a ring goes a long way to get a couple of favors done.) Anyway, they shot at us as we were running toward the water, but they missed and hit a Peruvian family. We stood there in the water taking in this horrific scene. There was blood everywhere. It dripped down the sand into the water. Suddenly, we saw a dorsal fin breach the waves, and then, a large, Great White shark jumped into the air and swallowed us.

There we were, sitting in this shark wondering how to get out. It didn't take long for us to realize that it was very comfortable inside of a shark, but we wanted to see what was above water. We fashioned a periscope out of some things we found, and poked it through the shark's blow hole. I'm not sure if you know, but sharks don't have blowholes, so we basically just stabbed the shark from inside and killed it.

The shark was taking on water. We got out of the shark and discovered we were "shark-wrecked" on a small island. It was a beautiful island inhabited by the Mbuti pygmy tribe. Who are the Mbuti pygmy tribe? Well, they are a kind people—a small and very smart people. Obviously, we put them to use to build up the island into a popular tourist destination.

Unfortunately, Ashley and I got into a fight over the naming of a new restaurant on the resort. I wanted "Sandysands" and Ashley wanted "Waterland." The fighting between us split the island down the middle, pitting families against families, brother against brother, dog against cat—a civil war ensued. All of the tourists fled and the pygmies killed each other. Ashley and I realized there were more important things in life than naming a restaurant. We hugged. Bygones became bygones.

Well, ladies and gentlemen, we had to dispose of the bodies somehow and thought that the most kind, civil way was to get a truck, load them up and drive it into the ocean, which we did. We got out of the truck and pushed it into the water, but got caught in a riptide and were dragged back in, with all of the bodies floating around us. We saw a dorsal fin breach the water and before we knew it, once again, we were in a shark. Ashley learned the shark's language and directed us here, to the island we are on right now. Welcome to the Hotel del Mar. Please beware of riptides.

MOON POOLS

gregory von Portz +
Ashley Rebecca King

A FIST FULL OF LOVE

Starring Ashley King and Greg Portz
"A Post-Modern Sonny and Cher"... Whatever That Means

Tuesday, September 5th
And
Thursday, September 7th
9:15 PM

$10 Cover Charge and $12 Food or Drink Minimum

Danny's Skylight Cabaret Room
346-348 W. 46th St. (Restaurant Row)
For Reservations Call
212.265.8130 or 212.265.8133

Catfish, Jazz and Eternity Converge

76

from *Inland Seagulls*
a book of short stories
by Gregory von Portz

We had what it was before anyone
else did. We all had "it," and we were
there for a reason. In the backwater of the
bayou stood a building called the Catfish
Motel. It wasn't so much known for its
sleeping accommodations as it was for its
bar. Hell, they didn't even serve catfish there.
It was just your plain, old, salted peanuts and
every Friday there was fried chicken. That's
it.

A winding road led to the motel. You
couldn't find it on a map if you tried. People
knew where it was though, and they came
every night of the week. All kinds of people
came. Nothing to do in the swamps, but
drink.

Voices sometimes came hollering
from down the woods. These were the people
who, after a day of fishing, would let it all
out. They lived on houseboats mostly. Their
temporary houses stuck permanently in the
mud. We called them "gulls". The gulls were
always flipping around looking to take a bite
out of someone or something.

Officer Childs would let us do an extra
ten minutes of music, if we brought some of
our friends in. This never happened to me. I
didn't have many friends. Al Mocher always
was bringing people in. He was the bringer.
Boy, he could play the horn real good. And

always got the most tips. He took an ad out in the newspaper and that's how he got all them people to come in. Al was smart like that. Can't hate that! I knew a good hustle when I saw one.

Al played jazz mostly, though he could play standards real good, too. His eyes would light up against his dark skin every time he blew. It was really something to see. Officer Childs liked Al.

Officer Childs wasn't a police officer anymore, not since he shot that Mexican son of a bitch who was fucking his wife. He shot her, too. Only in the foot, though. She can't really walk anymore. Lara was her name and she lived in room 17 of the motel. Officer Childs owned the place, and on account of him shooting her, he let her stay rent free.

The officer was also the bartender and ran the entertainment. He was real thin and always wore blue velvet jackets and had his head shaved. The shaved head made him look like a catfish.

The county was supposed to build a highway right through the swamp. Well, next to it at least. Officer Childs put up that motel right away thinking he could make a buck or three off tourism. Well, the highway never came. Too many workers died in the swamp. So there we all were at the Catfish Motel. Most of it was actually in the swamp. Big wooden stilts held everything up like a real, haphazard foundation. The bar hovered over the swamp, and if the room was empty you could hear the gators snapping for fish below.

That was the room we played in. Officer Childs knew how to run that place real good. The entertainment changed from night to night, except for the regulars: me, Al, Mary and Paps. Mary's act was to read verses from the Bible. Sometimes she'd put on a Beatles record, strip down to her panties and hoola hoop. She was young but looked old. Paps was the opposite of Mary. He was Officer Child's father and liked to play "A Bicycle Built for Two" on a kazoo. He'd just play that damn song over and over. He lived in room two, next to Officer Childs.

I lived in room 20, the last room on the edge of the swamp. It was small, but you didn't need much. Just quarters for the laundry machine, which Officer Childs rigged to charge a dollar instead of the regular fifty cents. As long as I sang, I could stay there.

"Castaways of Glory"

Portz & King, 2005

Mary's not a sinner
Bible Holy Roller
She likes to have her company
And she loses all control

In her room
Is a picture
Bottle caps & paper
What she does
She can do
But it can wait 'til later

A haiku
About winter
About changing with the seasons
In the spring
You can find her
Asking God for reasons

Mary's not a sinner
Matthew's not a savior

Matthew's not a savior
Drunk on Holy water
Sleeping in the heat of the day
Dreams of fields of potters

In his room
Is a painting
Tin cans & places
When he wakes
He'll atone
But he can't see the faces
A poem
About springtime
About blooming like a flower
In the fall
You can find him
Praying for some power

Matthew's not a savior
Mary's not a sinner
And she'll put you on a pedestal
She'll hang you up with cable
And she'll sacrifice her muses
On the kitchen table

There is thunder in laughter
There is silence in a warning
There are spirits in the rafters
There are people in the morning
Living in the moment
They will live that way forever
And forever and forever
And forever 'til the time's spent

Now they go down to the sand
Resting by the ocean
Waiting with each other
For the sea is bound to open
When it does
They can hear
The sound of their reflections
They hear the sounds of sighs
When the water starts to rise

Mary & Matthew
Castaways of Glory
They like to have their fun
But cannot tell the story
In the waves

The candles are dripping; the wax runs down the side like condensation on a glass of white wine on a hot summer's day. Dreamy plumes of steam search for a way to get to cooler air. There is no cool air. You don't like the cold. You hate the cold. Your shoulders tense and your breath gets shallow when you think about it. Sand between your toes and a drink in your hand is what you miss the most. It doesn't matter where. Croatia is as perfect as Mexico.

It's so snowy and freezing here in New York City, you wonder why you ever used your inheritance to rent a studio apartment on the Upper East Side. You know exactly why. Greg and Ashley lived on the Upper East Side when they first moved to New York. This fact was revealed in an interview and in one of their shows.

You've lived all over the world. Born in International Falls, Michigan, it must have been a foregone conclusion with a home town named like that. From Europe to Asia, from Eurasia to Indochina—no place felt like home. A visceral flashback throws you to the South China Sea. It's you taking a boat from Hong Kong to your new "home" in London. You were six and it was a whirlwind for your senses. Nothing so far has been able to compete with it except for maybe, no definitely, Moon Pools. Your travel style, skill, and breadth is beyond reproach. No one is quite like you, no one except for *them*.

They know what you're feeling; they've been thrown about the globe, too. If they know you, why don't they even acknowledge your existence? Huh? I guess they *are* too good. You've written letter after letter—nothing. It's OK. You'll still go to their shows, you'll buy their merchandise, you'll smile and clap. Maybe you'll get pulled onto the stage, like all of the other so called "fans!" Why do they get to do it and you don't? Is it your skin? Your ugly skin. Is it your breath? Goddamn it. It's probably your clothes. You should wear all-black clothing all of the time. You make a note of that.

Hot water burns your foot as you stick half of it in the water, then submerge your entire naked body in the scalding glory. *Heaven*. It's bathtime, no bubbles tonight. The walls, where you painted murals of Gregory von Portz and Ashley Rebecca King get heavy with moisture; the paint runs. King's face becomes smudged and melty like a plastic mask under a fast food heat lamp. The wax from the candles pools on the floor, it's warm and malleable like your muscles. You watch the blue wax from the "ocean-scented" candle dribble and collect. Why, with the light from the flame flickering, it looks like the moon is reflected off of a natural pool. You laugh to yourself as you watch the painted faces on your wall morph into gargoyles. The water is still hot as you submerge your ears to cloud the music you are playing. It's a bootleg of their show. The one you stood outside for four hours for.

Get out of the bath. You have to go.

They say that not all who wander are lost, but you're lost, thanks to those two and their fake cover band. After the bath, you travel the city in the cold. Moon Pools is playing at an ethnic restaurant, you're just not sure which one, or what kind.

Gina's Supreme Emerald House
Traditional Cantonese and Lobster

Tonight's Special:
THE EMPRESS'S POCKET
Large fish stuffed with crab, bok choy, jade, house-special pork fried rice

Appetizer Special:
Corn and Shrimp Balls (Spicy or Mild)

Drink Special:
Mandarin Mai Thai
(Special Mug add $5 deposit – refundable)

Live Performance TONIGHT ONLY

Portz & King: The Take-Away Tour
Sponsored by the Audubon Society of 55th Street

No cover
2 drink minimum

Please visit our other establishments:

MacArthur Park on Broadway
Fine Scottish Dining and Specialty Bakery

Lady Lee's of Harlem
Pigs Feet, Wings & Beer

Portz + King set
" Come On-a My House Mandarin
MacArthur Park
" Gimme a Pig Foot Canda Bottle of Beer

Item 421: Take-Away Tour Promo
Menu insert from Gina's Supreme Emerald House
231 East 55th Street - January 22nd

Gina's Supreme Emerald House

Traditional Cantonese and Lobster
<u>Tonight's Special:</u>

THE EMPRESS'S POCKET
Large fish stuffed with crab, bok choy, jade,
house-special pork fried rice

<u>Appetizer Special:</u>
Corn and Shrimp Balls (Spicy or Mild)
<u>Drink Special:</u>
Mandarin Mai Thai
(Special Mug add $5 deposit – refundable)

<u>Live Performance TONIGHT ONLY</u>

Portz & King: The *Take-Away* Tour
Sponsored by the Audubon Society of 55th Street

No cover
2 drink minimum
<u>Please visit our other establishments:</u>

MacArthur Park on Broadway
Fine Scottish Dining and Specialty Bakery
Lady Lee's of Harlem
Pigs Feet, Wings & Beer

Portz and King set list: (*handwritten*)
"Come On-A My House" (in Mandarin)
"MacArthur Park"
"Gimme a Pig Foot (And a Bottle of Beer)"

Former location of Gina's Supreme Emerald House

Moon Pools:

An Exclusive and Dynamic Interview with Our Heroes

*From a prominent Japanese magazine called **Prominence***

(Note: This cost $27 to have shipped from Tokyo)

をねえ。グレゴリー·フォン· Portzともムーンプールとして知られているアシュリーのレベッカ王は、日本-O-ファン雑誌で座った。彼らは、セントルイス、ミズーリ州に彼らの行為をもたらしていると何とか我々は、これらの2つの怠惰な白い人にインタビューしてしまった。

日本-O-ファン：
では、なぜアメリカ人はそう、脂肪怠惰な、とダムがありますか？

グレッグ·フォン· Portz ：
私は日本語を話せないすみません。

日本-O-ファン：
完全涼しい。

日本-O-ファン：
では、なぜアメリカ人はそう、脂肪怠惰な、
とダムがありますか？

グレッグ・フォン・Portz ：
私は日本語を話せないすみません。

日本-O-ファン：
完全涼しい。

日本-O-ファン：
では、なぜアメリカ人はそう、脂肪怠惰な、
とダムがありますか？

グレッグ・フォン・Portz ：
私は日本語を話せないすみません。

日本-O-ファン：
完全涼しい。

"WNDRRR"
Excerpt from Ashley's Diary
December 13th

WINDOWS
window
winddow
win dough
win no
WinDo
wndo
wndw window
win dow
win dow jones
wind o
whin doh
whine dow
wine doh
wined doh
wind dow
wnno
windr
wdr
wn
whn
wehn
when
do

I am tired of sitting here.

This is Really Reality, Kids.

by Gregory von Portz

Copied from *Dogs Don't Love, They Die*
an unpublished collection of
children's tales and games

The Itsy Bitsy spider stopped going to school.

The Itsy Bitsy spider got a job at the Piercing Pavilion in the mall.

Down went the economy and the mall closed.

And the Itsy Bitsy spider wished it had gone to higher education, but then saw their friend the Incy Wincy spider making smoothies next door, and remembered that Wincy went to school to be a doctor and graduated. The Itsy Bitsy spider then realized that education is a farce and it's what you make of it. And even if you have the knowledge of a doctor, it's sometimes hard to get a job in your field. That means you have to suck it up, be an adult and earn a living by any means possible, even if that means working at the Slush Shack making smoothies. That's what real, responsible people do: they make it work.

Moon Pools

October 27th Set List

"Kids In America"

"Shake Some Action"

"Ghost in You"

"Here"

"All the Young Dudes"/
 "Fake Plastic Trees"/ "Change"

"Need You Around"/ "Colors of the Wind"

"Mullet Head"

"Where'd You Go"

"Rollin' With My Homies"

Medley

"Tenderness"

"My Forgotten
 Favorite"

"Away"

"Shoop"

"Just a Girl"

"All By Myself"

"Perfect Day"

"Alright"

"We Are Young"

"I Try"

"Super Model"

a cold water flat – Upper East Side
New York City

The view from below - Little Arabia District, NYC

BACKLASH
Performed by Portz & King
Partial monologue transcribed from unauthorized audio recording

July 4th, New York City

Greg delivers monologue about their swift rise to stardom after moving to New York City.

GREGORY VON PORTZ:

Twelve years later, we were in NYC. You could find us working as costume characters in Times Square—you know, the dirty ones with the backpacks. The working conditions were horrible, so we tried to unionize. We wanted health care. It didn't work.

Ashley became a burlesque dancer and I played ukulele, but everyone is a burlesque dancer or plays ukulele. You don't even need talent to play the ukulele.
We had talent. We had BLUE-RIBBON TALENT!

Music cue Ashley only: "The Snake Charmer Song" (aka "The Streets of Cairo")

We got a job in the Little Arabia district of NYC. You may not have heard of Little Arabia before, but you certainly have smelled it. It lies somewhere along West 36th Street in the Garment District. You go down an alleyway next to huge spools of yarn. The alley is dark, damp and that's where the smell is coming from—black mold. It's suffocating you, so you run quickly. You see the light at the end of the tunnel, and are greeted with a burst of dry heat.

You're in a desert. You're in Little Arabia with sand, pyramids, snake charmers, markets, the noise and divine chaos. It's beautiful. In the center of this madness stands The Hotel Marrakech. With its turquoise marble facade, it contrasts the hot desert sand like a watery oasis.

Inside is a nightclub: The Oasis Lounge. Sometimes, we would play with only four people in the audience. They were thieves, smugglers, F.I.T. students and tourists looking to save some money on a hotel.

> **(Transcriber's note: Portz & King are now simulating a performance in the Oasis Lounge)**

Music cue Ashley only: "Istanbul (Not Constantinople)"

Ladies and gentlemen,
I'm Gregory von Portz! And this—this is the exotic and talented Ashley Rebecca King!
Two forks went missing from dinner, and the management asks that you please drop them in the return box after the show. There will be no charges pressed. No one will care. No one will bat an eye.

Also, if you could, keep the glasses off the stage. Last time I decided to do a barefoot dance, and had to get thirty-seven stitches in my foot.

Now that we have business out of the way, come with us to the most magical place on earth—To the Mediterranean Sea. To the Middle East. Or to whatever sea is in the Middle East.

Music Medley including:
"Istanbul (Not Constantinople)"
"Walk Like an Egyptian"

Reminder: Keep your glasses off the stage!

Music cue Ashley only: "Midnight at the Oasis"

We weren't just walking like Egyptians. We were walkin' like pharaohs. Moon Pools became quite popular. But it was bittersweet: you see, we always wanted a following of suicidal teenagers who would buy whatever we told them to buy. But our actual following was from Park Slope—people who lived in Brooklyn and acted like they lived on farms. Go to the grocery store! That's what it's there for! You wanna live on a farm? Get out of my fucking city.

The reviews were great: Ashley was described as "a young-looking Carly Simon." I was described as "a milquetoast, mild-mannered gentleman."

Our song stylings together were described as "Loud, always too loud." and "...akin to rape." Thank you, Broadwayworld.com.

(Transcriber's note: research actual review)

They gave us the New Year's Eve Show. All the elite of NYC and the worldly, international set were there. Gwyneth Paltrow was in attendance.

(Portz and King simulate the New Year's Eve performance at the Oasis)

Ladies and gentlemen, I'm Gregory von Portz and this is the beautiful, the wild, the exotic Ashley Rebecca King! We wish you all a happy New Year.

The management would like me to take this time to ask whoever stole the paintings from the bathroom, if they could please return them after the set. No questions will be asked.

And, guys, if you could please keep your glasses off the stage. Last week I was doing a can-can. A couple kicks there, a couple kicks here: a couple people lost their eyesight due to the glasses I kicked in their faces.

It's almost Midnight—

8-7-6-5-4-3-2-1

Music cue: "Midnight at the Oasis"

GREGORY VON PORTZ:

We became successful enough to purchase a TV. One night, we watched a documentary on PBS about the County Fair. It was almost too painful to view at first, because we lost the blue ribbon. We got the red one, but we don't need to get into that right now.

They interviewed two little girls; twelve years old, the same age Ashley and I were when we started performing at county fairs. They were twins, redheads with glasses

They looked a little familiar, a little like Kay Hollywood—the flute player.

Then they said their last name: Hollywood.

Holly-wood. Hollywood? I couldn't believe it.

They were Brianna and Janelle Hollywood, Kay Hollywood's children.

I saw blue.

Music cue Ashley only: "Egyptian Shumba" (menacing)

Ashley was so mad, she took the microwave and threw it out of the window.
I threw bleach on the walls and screamed. Then, I took that bottle of bleach and drank it. We took our favorite things and set them on fire. The whole apartment was on fire. The sirens and alarms were having a beautiful duet! Ashley and I ate the broken glass. Then the fire department arrived. But we had a show to do!

(Portz & King perform in the Oasis Lounge, slightly singed.)

Ladies and gentlemen! Welcome to the Hotel Marrakech. Now, stop stealing stuff or we will cut off your genitals! Get your fucking glasses off the stage! Shut the fuck up and listen!

Music cue: "Egyptian Shumba"

During the following number, Portz & King become increasingly more agitated, until Greg spots a painful reminder of their

failure adorning a member of the audience—
a blue ribbon on their hat— and they
completely lose control.

GREGORY VON PORTZ:

**(Transcriber's note: Inaudible screams
until the end)**

Music cue: silence

My good and lovely friends, have you ever
attacked an audience member?
Has anyone ever set a piano on fire and
shoved it into the audience maiming four
people?

Well, I can tell you that we have.

Oasis Fern

✱HOTEL *Marakesh*✱
NEW YORK CITY

Come see the Exotic International Personalities,
Gregory von Portz & Ashley Rebecca King
Performing Nightly at

THE OASIS LOUNGE

KEEP IN TOUCH. WE WANT TO SEE YOU AGAIN.

NAME: _____

EMAIL: _____

ADDRESS: _____

_____

PHONE: _____

THE OASIS LOUNGE AT THE HOTEL MARAKESH - LITTLE ARABIA, NEW YORK

Item # 130 Unused Courtesy Card
from the Hotel Marakesh

"Ancient roots -

or ancient routes?"

"Call Me a Cab"

Portz & King, 2004

We're sittin'
And chittin'
And chattin' all night long
You're mopin'
And I'm hopin'
I can keep my eyes open
You talk and
You're gabby
Why don't you just grab me?
You're pretty, but boring and drab

Throw me a bone
I don't like to be alone
You're such a clever lad
But I'd rather date a cad
So, I guess I'll just call me a cab

I'm waning
You're waxing
This could have been relaxing
You're quotin'
And emotin'
While you should be dotin'
You're jokin'
You're jokin'
It's me you should be strokin'
You're making me very mad

You must know it all from A to Z
With your pseudo-intellectual mentality

Oh.
You're touching me

Now we're sittin'
And kissin'
And blissin' all night long
I'm delighted
And excited
My love was requited
It's surprising
I'm reprising
This terminal endeavor
You're really not that bad

So, I'll put down the phone
I don't have to be alone
There's more fun to be had
And I think I should add
I won't have to call me a cab

I'm not gonna call me a cab.

Message in a Wine Bottle III

Dear Editor,

There is only so much rum two humans can drink before things go off the rails. Listen, editor, I'll be honest with you. We aren't on a desert island. We're on a small island somewhere in Polynesia performing in a low-grade Hotel del Mar knockoff resort. I mean, I guess it's deserted now ever since all of the locals left. (Read: Ashley forced them off with violence.)

Now, on to bigger and better stories. Many of our fans ask us, almost on a daily basis, "Why the obsession with beaches?" And sometimes I wonder myself. I feel especially horrible for Ashley, because she's allergic to salt water. Nevertheless, my heart will always be on the beach, like the still-beating hearts of the local people of this island were after Ashley vanquished them.

Some of you may remember the big blimp craze from a few years back. What a glamorous time to be alive. Airships crisscrossing the globe—it was like a cruise in the sky. Ashley and I were performing on the Gräffenberg Line, a German fleet of post-war zeppelins. They were gorgeous, painted all black with the most up-to-date modern conveniences the Germans could devise.

Every chair, bed, toilet, sofa and table had stirrups built in. I mean, leave it to the Germans to be able to build a secret basement with a torture chamber in the sky.

The inaugural flight was leaving from Frankfurt. We had a contract to do four shows a day, and were excited to get going. Over land and sea the Gräffenberg glided through the air like a spirit.

As we flew over the Tibetan Steppe, nearly brushing the ground at the top of the world, we could see the horses running. Wild, free, making ancient lines across the moss-green grass. Yurts dotted the landscape like those candies that were stuck to paper and you'd have to pull off, but you'd always get a piece of paper, but then you thought, fuck it. Only the yurts were white.

I dreamt that I was Genghis Khan and Ashley was Borte, his wife. Together we rode on the open land hand-in-hand, terrorizing the known world. Gracelessly, we slaughtered. Joyously, we sang covers of the popular songs of the day. Wild horses and domesticated yaks, we smelled of both. The trade routes called to Borte. She wanted to escape from this crazy Mongolian lifestyle. She loved me, but had to go. I let her. As she took her horse to the horizon, through tall and fragrant grass, the coins she fastened to her hair glistened. I had her slaughtered.

107

The air smells different when you are up there in it. Temperature doesn't exist; you can only tell what the climate is by looking at the foliage on the ground. Several of the occupants of the craft succumbed to cabin fever or a stomach virus. No one can point a finger for the cabin fever, but let's just say that Ashley likes to take sips from strangers' drinks a little too much.

Regardless, to cheer up the passengers and crew, we had a surprise show. We called it *Air Surprise!* The finale involved a big fireworks display.

Sadly, the blimp caught on fire and fell to earth in a blaze of German-made glory. Luckily, we were in the arctic; I'm not certain which one—ant or regular. You see, the zeppelin fell faster than Ashley and I, and it hit the snow, melting it and turning the area beneath us into a pool.

The water froze around us. And there we were, in suspended animation—Moon Pools: On Ice. While the rest of the world mourns climate change, we bless it, for it thawed us out after several years and let us continue our work as a cover band.

So, the next time someone asks why Moon Pools only does shows where it's warm, have them buy a copy of this book or buy one for them. Then highlight the story above.

Kindness is edgy,
Gregory von Portz

A very cold night

Live from New York City

Alpha Psi Omega Presents

In A
Polynesian
Mood

Starring~Gregory von Portz
and Ashley Rebecca King

McKelvey, Berlin Lounge
9:00 PM Friday, April 9th

Presented as part of
Westminster College's
2010 One Act Festival

* For Audiences 18 and over

Original Ad by Graham McCarthy

Item # 410 Artistic Interpretation of Tour Poster.
No actual copies saved.

Sometimes the spring air is so intoxicating, you feel like you could jump off a building. But tonight, you're not going to do that. You'd never do that. In death, there's no Moon Pools. Nope, not you.

You took a surrey cart to where you are right now. You felt bad for the person pushing the surrey since it was across the entire state of Pennsylvania. The vehicle surrey-ed through the natural majesty that is Interstate 80. Trees gave way to trees, which gave way to more trees. Occasionally, you and the surrey cart driver would talk about life and longings.

Eating pre-packaged meals day after day of the seventy-nine hour journey was exhausting. You just took a nap in the hotel room. The sheets, crisp and perfumed, made you feel good. The room is beautiful: just a deck of cards and bottle of brandy, it's enchanting. A nervous pang crawls up your body. You're gonna get caught. Yes, this hotel room is beautiful but it's not yours—it belongs to Gregory von Portz and Ashley Rebecca King.

You got into the room by wearing your best Ashley costume. The front desk staff didn't say anything when you said, "I forgot my room number. Oh, and can I have my key? Please." You ran quickly to room 68. Yippee! You were in. Now, they wouldn't be back for five hours. You knew this, because you bribed their roadie with weed to tell you their itinerary. Greg's smell lingers on the bed. The socks, you're sure are Ashley's, are now in your mouth. If only they could see you like this, then they'd bring you up onstage.

You take a long bath using their products. You're allergic to most of them. You light up a cigarette and drink a glass of wine.

Ashley and Greg are playing at a small college. You won't get to see this show. There are more important things to do, like sleeping in Greg's bed, for example. You would have slept in Ashley's bed, but she sleeps in the bathtub—to save money.

This is better than seeing their show. You're seeing their life. Their souls.

Your hands start rifling through their stuff. This is way easier than you imagined. You find Ashley's diary and some notebooks.

You collect them.

Champagne Toast at the Oasis Lounge- Little Arabia,
New York City

An Article from *Back That Up*

A magazine by and for back-up singers

Not to Sound 'Cliché' But Don't Call it a Comeback

Famed back up trio—minus two— makes a comeback.

by Alec J. Smith

Yes! They're back and better than ever. After a two-year hiatus, and the death of two of its three members, Cleo and the Clichés—the world's best back-up singing trio—is back up on its feet (except for the two members who died in horrible ways).

This Friday, at the Spencer Miller Pavilion in Century Park at the county fair, they'll be back. The two members who died tragically will be replaced by random audience members. Not only were the dead women her sisters, they were like family to lead singer Cleo Cleaveaux.

Originally from Detroit, the trio climbed their way up the ranks of the Motown girl group ladder to land at the very middle rung. Even at the height of their careers, the trio worked 9-to-5 jobs: one as an attorney, one as a lawyer (those two died), and Cleo as a doctor.

We caught up with Cleo—the titular and only surviving member of the group—she's happy to be back. "These mother (expletive) haven't seen the last of me. I'mma be singing up a mother (expletive) storm on that stage. After my sisters died in a terrible foldable cot accident, I haven't been able to sing—on account of the alcoholism and prescription drug abuse."

Most will remember Cleo and the Clichés as the back-up singers for Gregory von Portz and Ashley Rebecca King while they toured the world in their fake cover band Moon Pools. Others will remember them as the sister act where two of them died in a cot when it snapped shut like a mouse trap.

Of her time with Portz and King Cleo says, "Those mother (expletives) didn't pay us a (expletive) penny that I could rub my (expletive) on. I would have made more money if I went out on the track and (expletive) for fifty cents a (omitted) job. They were always dragging us around, and we had to pay for our own hotel rooms. It was ridiculous. We were, like, kidnapped by them and treated like common garbage. But we did it for the love of singing back-up." Cleo writes extensively about this time in her life in her book, *I, Cleo, Take the Stage of Life and All of its Amenities*. The book has been said to read like a "who's that?" of the music industry.

Cleo continued after several drinks, "Then Ashley and Greg come to my sisters' funeral. And you know what they did? Sang a goddamned mother (expletive) song about death. It was the biggest funeral Detroit has seen, and then they had to take all of the attention like they always do with everything. There they were up there singing. They looked really thin and had good complexions, but they were singing an inappropriate song at my sisters' funeral!"

If you can't make it to the county fair, you can catch Cleo and the "new" Clichés in an as-yet-to-be-filmed documentary called *Two Tragic Deaths and a Girl Group.*

Item # 509

"Ah, a Little Death"

Portz & King, 2009

*Transcribed from cell phone video footage taken at
the "Cliché" funeral and downloaded off the internet.*

Ah, a little Death
Ah, a little Life
Your soul is a kite on a string
A little wrong
A little right
You know what the future will bring
And that's
Demise
The obliteration
Of everything you've ever known
'Cause we all live together
But we all die alone

A little life
A little death
Your heart sometimes leads you astray
A little right
A little left
We can't stop it when it gets in our way
But hearts decay
And so will we
Until we're dust and bones
For we all live together
But we all die alone

We're all gonna die someday
Even if you're good... or pretty
Time will take you anyway
That's why I'm singin' this little ditty

Oh, A little death
Oh, A little death
Your body ends up in the ground
Oh, there's nothing left
There's nothing left
There's not a cure to be found
And that's for death
The end of everything
She's coming to carry me home
EVERYBODY!
'Cause we all live together
But we all die alone

We all live together
We all die
alone!

"Many people told me to kill myself. I won't give them the satisfaction."

Man with One Eye

by Gregory von Portz

Copied from *Dogs Don't Love, They Die*
an unpublished collection of
children's tales and games

There is a man
With just one eye,
Spends his days down by the creek.

Watching garbage float by
With his one eye,
He looks at the water, but doesn't speak.

Bunny is the lady who sings in the church
She has that bouffant hair.
One day she was throwing rotten apples in
the creek,
And saw the one-eyed man sittin' there.

She said "I saw you winkin'
        And I was thinkin'
I was gonna blush until I die."
He said, "I'm real flattered m'am,
        But seeing as I am
I wasn't winkin',
        I've only got one eye."

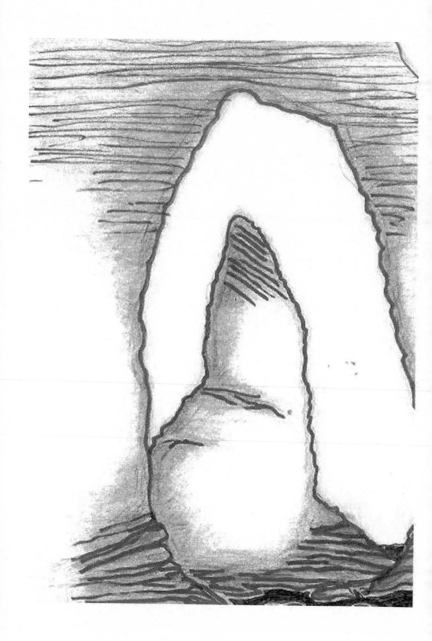

I AM ON AN ISLAND

A LAND WITH
NO TREES,

NO BEACHES -

"Red Sails in the Sunset"
A Junk Boat - Hong Kong, China

Maybe you can stop by their hotel? The Hotel del Huo. (That's Hotel del Mar in Mandarin) You know where it is. You've been to all of their shows. Remember? They'd know your name. Yeah. Greg and Ashley are good, nice people who love their fans. They have to know your name. You haven't been on stage yet—they need to drag you up there first. Ha. You'd pretend that you don't want to be brought up, but you'd eventually let go of control and give over to complete rapture. And then - and then you'd be on stage at a Moon Pools show. **Calm down**.

If you see them at the hotel, you could tell them that you've been transcribing their shows and collecting Moon Pools memorabilia. Yeah, they'd be cool.

The rickshaw with Hotel del Huo written on the side picks you up at the airport. The driver is silent as he pulls you along the coast of the South China Sea. Ahead, the lights of Hong Kong shine bright and reflect off of Victoria Harbour. You remember when you spent time here, as a child. It doesn't even feel like home. You can never go home.

You're here. This is it. The venue is supposed to be intimate, and that's perfect for you. You want to catch their eye during a medley, or maybe the opening number. There's this fantasy you have of the both of them hoisting you onto the stage: You're singing "Bridge Over Troubled Water" as Ashley plays the piano, and a gospel choir appears out of nowhere to sing along with you—with Moon Pools.

Hong Kong Island is a more vibrant place than you remember from the time you spent here as a six-year-old. The Ding-Ding trams are humming like your heart. You get on a boat that will take you to the beach where Moon Pools is performing.

While most of the boats are brand new, your boat is an old junk boat with red accordion sails. The water is a deep turquoise. Your reflection dances in the ripples. You take a sip from your flask.

Fog rises off of the city behind you, as your heart pumps like an oil rig sucking from the earth. You take another swig of your flask. It's pure vodka. You like to feel everything. You especially like to feel the things you drink. Your throat burns as the sun burns the clouds away. Before you, a small island breaks through the waning mist.

A fishing village, you think to yourself. How quaint. A surrey cart is waiting for you, and it whisks you off to the venue. The place is packed. You see the door that clearly says "BACKSTAGE." Go for it, you must.

You run through the crowd of Australians and Chinese and get to the door. A thin, imposing, young-looking woman wearing all black and with the slightest Southern drawl says, "I'm sorry you can't go in there." It's Elizabeth, their manager. She's been with them through thick and thick. Why, she's even seen Greg cry on a bare mattress in his underwear. (She's seen Ashley cry too, but had the good sense to throw a jar of change at her.) You knew she existed, but didn't know she'd be this serious.

Out of nowhere you are being chased by a dog. His name is Petri and he is the cutest chihuahua you've ever seen, but he is vicious and chasing you. You know he is the Moon Pools attack dog.

Catching your breath, you can hear the show going on in the distance. Ha. You are missing it. The whole thing. What you traveled miles and spent so much money on you are now missing. You feel something inside of you, something that screams, shrieks, "Hate them like they hate you. You'll never be brought up on stage in a Moon Pools show. Stop trying, and make them pay."

You hate them.

You hate Gregory von Portz and Ashley Rebecca King.

You loathe them.

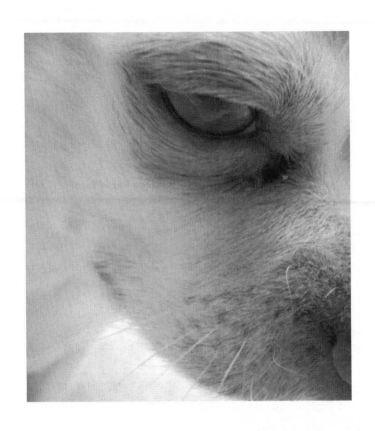

Petri

AUTHORITIES HUNT FOR FAMED ARCHITECT, KIDNAPPED

By Dr. Richard Smith, Ph.D.

Maui-Hawaii: Famous hotel architect, Susan Darrow, has been reported missing by her daughter, Ally. Security footage from her Maui home shows a single person breaking in late at night. Neighbors said they heard a struggle, but assumed someone was watching TV.

Darrow is known as the architect for the now defunct chain of cheap, Polynesian-themed hotels named *Hotel del Mar*.

Item # 917

Waiting for the morning star

Message in a Wine Bottle IV

Dear Editor,

It was odd—the way the boat just sank. There wasn't a warning, just a mystery person hiding in shadows. Then, there was the squeaking of dolphins. Hundreds of them. As the ship took on water, that sound was replaced with the screaming of people onboard. How I miss the cheers of an audience.

Thankfully, our major set piece—a giant moon—was buoyant. Now, I'm sure you're wondering if there were women and children aboard. And I'm sure you're wondering if we saved any of them. The answer is yes and no. No, because we are nothing if not progressive with our views on gender roles. Everyone is equal. In fact, Ashley wrote a book called "Gender Rolls" about baking, no matter what gender. It didn't sell very well.

There we were out on the high sea with nothing but a piano. We used the piano wires to catch fish. We caught tons of fish. It was a miracle, actually. There are indeed plenty of fish in the sea. At one point, they started jumping into the vessel. Unfortunately, neither Ashley nor I eat fish, and they just stayed right there and rotted on the deck.

Alas, here we are now, and Ashley has fashioned an oven out of sea glass, wet palm fronds and an old stove she found on this very deserted island. Currently, she's making hot cross buns.

Kindness is Edgy,
Gregory von Portz

The Famous Moon - created in exile by G. McCarty

Ashley's Recipe for *Rockin' Roti*

From *Gender Rolls: a cookbook for the gender neutral*

Ingredients:

1 cup flour (white or wheat)

½ cup water

½ tsp salt

Lots of oil

Instructions:

Combine flour and salt in a bowl. Slowly add water, mixing with hands, and knead until smooth. Let sit for 15 minutes, then separate into small balls, and roll out using a rolling pin or beer can.

Heat oil on the stove. Cook 1 roll at a time, flipping when it starts to bubble to cook on other side.

Monitor and keep flame at medium or you will burn down your friend's apartment.

Holy Moses

A one-act play by Gregory von Portz

Rejected submission for theater festival
of Bible-based one-act plays

<u>SCENE</u>
A delta.

<u>TIME</u>
A time of oppression.
A summer morning.

<u>ACT I</u>
<u>Scene 1</u>

(Music "Border Song" by Aretha
Franklin thru first verse.)
(LIGHTS BACK ON)

A phone rings

JO

    (on phone)
How d' do? 'Batt, Calm down—calm
down.
Moses? My baby Moses?
Well, he's right here being all
cute. No. I didn't see anything
on the news.
Pharaoh's gonna do what? To whom?
Oh, hell no. Throw my baby in the
river!?

135

(Cut to the PHARAOH's house)

PHARAOH
I decree that we shall throw
babies in the river, because
without children we don't have
to worry about the future.

(JOCOBETH's Living room)

JO
Damn. Damn. Damn.
What do I do? What do I do? Can
anyone help an Israelite out?

GOD
Psst...

JO
Who is it?

GOD
Throw it down the river.

JO
Throw what down the river?

GOD
Your baby...down the
river...makes sense to me.

JO
Who is this?

                    GOD
God.

                    JO
I don't know, God. I'll think
about it.

        (Cut to JO's THOUGHT PROCESS)

            THE THOUGHT PROCESS
Um. I'd go with God on this one.

                    JO
Ok, I'll do it. Miriam! Get down
here right now.

             (MIRIAM enters)

                  MIRIAM
Mom! I was listening to music.

                    JO
Something is wrong with you.

                  MIRIAM
Whatever. I'm gonna go back
upstairs to talk on the phone
with my boyfriend.

                    JO
Damn that. Put some clothes on! I
have a plan.

                    137

(Ten minutes later)

                    MIRIAM
Mom, this isn't a good idea.

                      JO
I don't care what you think. I am
so mad at you right now. I told
you NOT to bring my good picnic
basket.

                    MIRIAM
This isn't a good idea.

                      JO
YES IT IS.

                    MIRIAM
No. It's not

                      JO
Yes.

                    MIRIAM
No.

                      JO
Yes!

                    MIRIAM
NO!

                    JO
Yes! Now, let's drop that thing
in and run.

              (One hour later
          farther down the river)

                THERMUTHIS
Geez. Bathing in the river is
fun and all, but I wish I wasn't
barren.
What's this? A baby. Thank you,
Ramesses.

            (JOCOBETH's apartment
              ten minutes later)

                    JO
Oh, I think I made a mistake. I
think I made a mistake. Do you
think I made a mistake, Miriam?

                  MIRIAM
Yes.

                    JO
What?

                  MIRIAM
Yes.

                    JO
No.

                  MIRIAM
<u>Yes</u>.
You threw my baby brother down
the river in a basket!

                    JO
My good basket!

                  MIRIAM
Listen, I followed the basket and
saw Pharaoh's daughter or wife or
something pick it up. He probably
has him.

                    JO
Let's go!

            (PHARAOH's office)

                  SECRETARY
 Thank you for calling, Pharaoh's
office...
 Wait, I'm sorry you can't go in
there.

          (Inside of the office)

                  PHARAOH
Yes. How may I help you two?

                    140

                    JO
You have my baby!
I threw it down the river.

                 PHARAOH
Finders keepers.

                    JO
Damn. You got me there!
Miriam, he got me with that one!

                  MIRIAM
Mom, stop. You're embarrassing
me.

                 PHARAOH
Listen, let's just cut him in
half.

                    JO
Ok.

                 PHARAOH
Just kidding woman. Why don't I
keep him and you can breastfeed
him?

                    JO
Deal!

                  MIRIAM
Oh, God....

                    141

GOD

Yes....?

JO

Sometimes, it is like you are
reaching for something out there
but...

(Music cue: "Unwritten")

Item #918

MOON POOLS: The Gospel of the Holidays Set List

OPENING: Holiday Medley
"Sleigh Ride"
"What Christmas Means to Me"
"This Hanukkah"
"Step Into Christmas"
"We Don't Have to Take Our Clothes Off"
"8 Days of Christmas"

Greg's Monologue: It doesn't feel like Christmas…
"We Three Kings"
"Somewhere in My Memory"
"God Rest Ye Merry Gentlemen"
"I Saw Three Ships"
"Carol of the Bells"
"Joy to the World"
"The First Noel"

"Salvation Army Song"

MEDLEY: "The Christmas Shoes"
"Life in a Northern Town"
"We Found Love
"Halo"

"Celebrate Me Home"

"Christmas Wrapping"

Greg's Monologue: Story of the Mistletoe, a Norse Myth
"Winter"
"Last Christmas"
"Let It Snow"

"Grandma Got Run Over by a Reindeer" /"My Favorite Things"

Moon Pools Giveaway!
Name That Tune with one note
(Ashley only) = "Jingle Bells"

Greg reads a Christmas Card:
"Christmas Card from a Hooker"

CHRISTMAS SPECTACULAR FINALE
(Featuring the Von Portz Family Singers)

"Christmas (Baby, Please Come Home)"
"I'll be home for Christmas"
"Joy to the World"
"Oh, Happy Day"
"Ants Marching"
"Do They Know It's Christmas"
"Hark! The Herald Angels Sing"
"We Don't Have to Take Our Clothes Off"
"All I Want for Christmas is You"
"I Try"

Item #256 – Set list
Moon Pools Holiday Show

Photos on page 143
(Top to bottom)
Performing "The Gospel"
On a Stay-Cation
Performing at Westminster

"I once threw myself down an icy hill to try and break my ankle to get out of school.

It didn't work. I got out of school, but my ankle remained intact."

The Old Rugged Hostel

This Little Light of Mine

C F C
C F G
C B/Am G F

Am G C

Jones Town
Change Key to Bb (2b)
(Eb Bb)

Bb A#(not or #) (G Bb A#) F Eb w3b
(b)

G (Bb Eb (Bb) Bb Ab/Bb (F)(Am)

Bridge
G (Bb) Bb Fm F#

Dmm Eb/Bb

Item #21: Ashley's discarded notes
Salvaged November 14th

BACKLASH

Performed by Portz & King

Partial monologue transcribed from
unauthorized audio recording

July 4th, New York City

**Music cue Ashley only:
"Midnight Train to Georgia"**

GREGORY VON PORTZ:

After we saw Briana and Janelle Hollywood
on television, drank bleach, burned our
apartment, performed to a sold-out crowd—
which we threw a flaming piano into—were
subsequently arrested, tried for the murder
of a person we crushed with said piano and
then convicted, we got a plea bargain. As part
of the terms of this plea bargain, we were
forced, or I like to say "asked" to turn
ourselves in to a mental
institution/sanatorium in the Blue Ridge
Mountains of Georgia.
You can only imagine how... excited we were.
Neither of us had ever been below the
Mason-Dixon line. Since we were young
we've been working and puttin' on shows.
This was the vacation we never asked for.

Hearing the phrase "the South" conjures a lot
of images for us: family gatherings, big
mansions with wrap-around porches, mint

juleps, sweet tea, girls in gingham dresses on a warm summer evening and racism.

You know how people surprise each other for big trips? Like, let's say for an anniversary a husband takes his wife to Paris. But first, he blindfolds her on the way to the airport so she's surprised once they get to the gate.

We wanted that experience. So, we blindfolded each other.

Neither of us had ever been on a plane before, and, as you can imagine, this was a pretty big deal for us. Ashley thought it was nice to be blindfolded. She has always enjoyed it. Not being able to see where you are has always been one of her very favorite travel tips. However, there was a problem with wearing blindfolds—we had to get to the airport. It was a nightmare - just us walking around on the highway trying to "feel" our way there.

We got to the terminal, got on an airplane, and the plane took off.
Ladies and gentlemen, the first time you fly, it's like going on a boat, or ship or something. You're just rocking back and forth. For us, the whole experience was heightened since we still couldn't see a damned thing.

But it really reminded me of being on a ship.

Three days went by and we hadn't landed. I had to, pardon my language, pee. I took my blindfold off.

It turns out we were actually on a ship, a big wooden ship filled with animals. We had "felt" our way to the regular port, instead of the air-port.

The captain and owner was named Old McDonald. He was an animal hoarder. The ship was filled to the brim will all sorts of animals. The smell was so pungent, so gamey that even Ashley couldn't handle it. And then the animal dung.... (Greg gags.)

Old McDonald didn't have a farm, he had a major health violation. But valderi, valdera. There we were on a ship full of all kinds of animals.

Music cue Ashley only: "Sea Shanty"
One of the animals on the ship was a pig wearing aviator goggles. We called him Goggles! He was so cute!

Music cue Ashley only: "Storm"
One morning, right before breakfast, the ship was listing back and forth, to and fro. (Greg gags.)

Ashley was getting seasick, so she drank whiskey—to calm her stomach. I went up on deck to check out the situation. The waves were seventy stories high. It wasn't the perfect storm, but it would do.

One wave came and took Old McDonald from the steering wheel, or whatever it's called.

I watched in horror as Goggles ran for shelter. I lost my sister in a freak storm at sea; I wasn't about to let the cutest pig I ever did see die the exact same way, too. And this little piggy jumped right into my arms. I held him as a giant wave broke across the ship. Then, my entire life passed before my eyes:

> Maybe I shouldn't have gotten all those people pregnant by passing out faulty condoms.

> Maybe I shouldn't have tried to burn down the school.

> Maybe I shouldn't have locked my parents in the basement and left them there, never to be heard from again.

Maybe, maybe, maybe, maybe.

Maybe I'm born with it. Maybe it's your past.

Music cue: "Border Song"

It's just your past. You can't worry about that when death is staring you in the face.

I prayed to the only biblical figure I knew of at the time: my dear friend, Moses.

Greg and Ashley perform "Border Song."

GREGORY VON PORTZ:

(Praying to Moses over instrumental music.)

Moses, listen: if you get me out of this one I will be a better person. I won't try to kill anymore; I won't rejoice at the deaths of my enemies; I'll say "thank you" when people open the door.
I will stop hating people. I will even stop hating redheads!

Greg and Ashley begin the last chorus of the song, which is interrupted by a crash.

A Holiday in the Canyon
Excerpt from Ashley's Diary
April 10th

As the two women made their way down the crooked path, the last amber rays of daylight splashed over the steep wall of pink rocks to their right and spilled down onto their sensible, orthopedic shoes.

"I think I might see a good spot ahead," announced Patty as she gingerly sidestepped a small, suspicious-looking pile of stones. They had learned quickly within the past few hours that unwholesome critters sometimes made their homes in such dwellings, and she had no desire to reenact the earlier incident. Patty, in fact, didn't mind most animals, but Linda had developed quite the aversion to all God's creatures after her son had been killed in a bull-riding incident nearly fifteen years ago. Patty still remembered the day vividly. The receptionist, who was new, had taken the message while Linda was out at lunch and, not knowing who Brandon was, callously left it written on the "While You Were Out" notepad they kept by the bookbinder. Patty herself discovered it while putting together presentations for the afternoon meeting and had to break the news to Linda. Linda was devastated by the passing of her only child, but put on a brave face and continued about her afternoon duties, mainly because the Jennings brothers, their employers, had no tolerance for displays of emotion of any kind, and also they requested coffee be made for the boardroom. Looking back, Patty knew there must have been some good days at work, but she was having trouble remembering those now. Anyway, it didn't matter anymore.

Linda, slightly ahead of Patty, paused to switch her over-sized, quilted hobo-bag from her right shoulder to her left. Shielding her eyes from the sun, she stole a glance at the sky and thought she could make out the faint, moving shadows of their tour group lumbering back toward the trail entrance, several yards above them. But her eyes were tired and hadn't been trustworthy for years, so it might have been more trees.

"I wasn't expecting the donkeys. You were so clever getting rid of them, Patty."

When they had arrived for the tour with a dozen other participants, they were alarmed to discover donkeys waiting for them. This was an obstacle they had not prepared for, but Patty, ever-resourceful, made loud complaints about her hip and inability to ride. Their guide insisted that a hike down the steep trail would be far more taxing, and even suggested that perhaps it was best if the ladies "sat this one out", but Linda and Patty, highly experienced in reasoning with even the smallest of minds, wore him down until they were permitted to follow behind on foot. It was clear that their guide, a man in his twenties, had no use for

154

the women, but they didn't mind. They'd become accustomed to such treatment.

"I knew we were out the minute we got that single-serve coffee maker," Patty had said on their last day of work. The women were let go from their positions on a bright spring day, with very little ceremony. The new office manager did order a cake made from cupcakes reading "Happy Retirement," but for Linda, a diabetic, this only served as a reminder of her soon-to-be-unpaid medical expenses.

When the ladies exited the newly-renovated building lobby, they each carried a box containing (in total) two small plants, three picture frames, a daily calendar about bunnies and a pile of clippings featuring quotes from that show they both liked about an office. They made a joint decision halfway down the block to dispose of these few possessions in the nearest trash receptacle and have a late lunch at the diner on the corner. That was where they began forming the plan.

It hadn't been hard to lose the tour group. As their guide casually rambled on about rock formations and aboriginal gods, they quietly slipped down a side trail and out of view. In their tote bags they carried plenty of water, some cans of tuna and warm clothes for the evening. Their biggest moment occurred when Linda stumbled over a pile of flat pebbles and out popped a monstrously large spider. The women were frightened at first, but they soon out-maneuvered the beast and Patty flicked him over the side with a stick. It was then that they realized they would be okay. This was an environment they could master.

The light was nearly gone now, as Linda rifled through her bag, locating a small pen light, the glow from which would illuminate the short distance that remained between them and the small abri Patty had spotted ahead. Once inside, they unpacked their bedding: two travel pillows and a pair of brightly-colored Mexican blankets they'd purchased at a nearby truck stop. They spread these neatly on the ground several feet from the entrance, side-by-side.

They were hungry, but they agreed it was a bad idea to eat here where they would sleep, not knowing what other kind of wildlife roamed about. The cave was shallow, more like a nook. The back wall was visible and strongly built. But still, this would not stop something ravenous from walking in on them. Besides, they'd eaten a can of tuna each only a few hours ago, hiding from the sun under a brittle tree. They briefly considered playing cards, but that would require light, and this, too, could draw unwanted attention. In the end, Patty admitted she was tired enough for bed, and Linda, who had gone camping as a girl, volunteered to take first watch. The stars came out as the women claimed their positions, filling the sky with a million tiny dots of fearsome light.

"I'll wake you in four hours," Linda said, propping her back against the cool mouth of the cave.

"Yes," said Patty as she began to drift away. "We made good progress today, and we shall go even farther tomorrow."

Elysium

Message in a Wine Bottle V

Dear Editor,

I hope you are getting these letters, faithful editor. Once we get off of this island, I would like a book published. I'd like it to have our logo on the cover and reviews on the back. Like a real book. I'd love to have a book launch party and a show at one of our more intimate spots in New York City. Above all, I'd like to make money with the book. I doubt we'll get money for our cruise ship contract. I remember there being a clause that if the ship sank we didn't get money or something.

Anyway, what a fun time we're having on the island. I've lost at least forty pounds and Ashley has really built up a lot of muscle from carrying all of the things she needs to carry—like our piano. Oh, did I tell you she fixed it? All she used was coconuts and now we have a piano! We can perform. There's just no one here to see it.

I love island life. It's so relaxing. I'm really scared. It feels like someone is watching us. Every day I think I'm having a mental breakdown, and I'm sickened to think that our fans will never get to pay money to see us again. Please send help.

I knew we should have never taken that cruise contract. I just knew it. When we were on the ship, I felt like we were being watched and I remember a shadowy character always lurking. Am I going crazy, Cheryl?

I don't want to scare Ashley, but I think she feels the same way, too. Please, find us! Help. SOS. We're in danger, I fear.

Kindness is edgy,
Gregory von Portz

They are powerless. You might never get up on stage with them. You don't give a fucking fuck. Those fuckers will pay. How much money did you spend on seeing their fucking shitty shows in basements? Basements? You were in a Murray Hill basement. That's not how you planned your life.

Stop laughing. Someone will see you and know. They'll know that you've spent several years of your life wasting your time. Well, you're about to stop wasting your time now. Everything is in place. You even bought a defunct cruise line and renamed it after Ashley's favorite bird. You are really smart and a genius.

That woman trapped in the closet won't stop yelling.

How to Plan a Party for Children
by Gregory von Portz

Copied from *Dogs Don't Love, They Die*
an unpublished collection of
children's tales and games

One of our most cherished memories is of
Moon Pools performing at a little girl's Sweet
Six party. It was fun to be on the receiving
end of questions
from children:

Why don't you get a real job?
Why are you here?
I don't know that song?
Who's Nina Simone?
Is your hair really blonde?
This is too much for me.
Can I go to the bathroom now?
Why are you screaming at me?
Why don't you get yourself together?
Stop yelling.
You are scaring me.

My question to them was, simply: Why are
you alive?

What made this party really
special was knowing that
someday these children
would be over-weight and
their blood would be as heavy
with sugar as honey.

162

How to have a Moon Pools-style Children's Party

Don't have children.
Spend money on vacations.

Ashley's Recipe for Moon Pools Punch party beverage (not for children)

Ingredients:

Large container of sherbet, any color/flavor

Gallon of Lemon-Lime soda

2 huge jugs of fake fruit juice (store brand is fine)

Ice

Alcohol of any kind (partial to flavored rum)

Instructions:

Mix all ingredients together. Serve after everyone's already drunk.

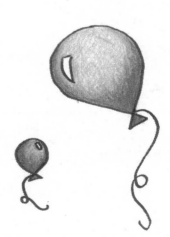

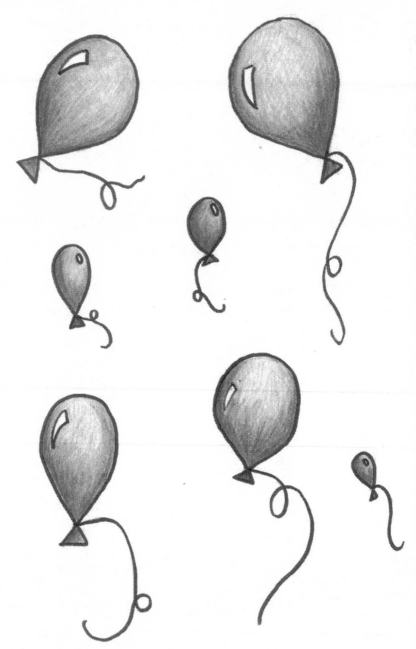

MOON POOLS TAKES MANHATTAN (Set List)

OPENING MEDLEY

"Sing"

"You Can Call Me Al"

"That's Not My Name"

"We All Sing With The Same Voice (My Name Is You)"

"Sing"

MONOLOGUE

"Somebody Come and Play"

"Hola"

"People in Your Neighborhood" – Drug Cartel

"Me and Julio Down By the School Yard"

"Rubber Duckie"

"Moving Right Along"

"Can You Picture That?"– Audience forced to take photos

"The 1st Time It Happens"–Audience Forced to act song

MOON POOLS GIVEAWAY: "Sing What I Sing"

NUMBERS AND TIME MEDLEY

"Pinball Countdown"

"1234"

"I'm Gonna Always Love You"

"What You Waiting For?"

"I'm Going to Go Back There Someday" (Ashley)

"Rainbow Connection"

WALK-ON ROLE AND FINALE MEDLEY

"Put Down the Duckie"

"Jump"

"A New Way to Walk"

"Love Led Us Here"

"Electric Youth"

"Dance, Magic, Dance"

"Together Again"

"I Try"   (Ashley's note: Greg says must change font)

Item #377: Ashley's set list

"I'm no doctor, but sometimes when someone's heart gives out, I think that's a conscious decision. You hear those stories of parents having heart attacks at the wheel with their children in the car. Well, maybe, they were done— just done with their bratty little children singing songs. They were finished. And there's no evidence."

THE FOREST OF DAMP

The Forest of Damp
by Gregory von Portz
Copied from *Dogs Don't Love, They Die*
an unpublished collection of
children's tales and games

Up over hills and valleys,
dark city alleys,
Past tundra
and sand,
and swamps
Is a place that is clean,
a place that is green.
It's a place called the forest
The Forest of Damp

The forest is humid,
a humid location.
The kind that you'd feel on a tropical
vacation.

It's the kind of place, you'd be safe to bet,
That's not as hot as warm,
and not as soaked as—well, wet.

Down past the bushes,
the bristle,
the brustle,
slept a family of bears
not moving a muscle.
The family was sleeping
at two past noon.
These bears just didn't want to get up too
soon.

Now they were quite lazy,
but very well off.
Sometimes they were mistaken
For being too sloth.

Their last name was Smith.
Yes, that's what it was
Don't ask me why.
I'll tell you:
"Well...'cause."

The Smiths loved the damp
They just breathed it in.
It was good for the nails,
and good for the skin.

Good for the liver,
and good for the lungs.
Good for the worms in the deepest of dung.

The Forest of Damp
would be their home for all time.
They loved the location—
and low instance of crime.

Mr. Smith was smart.
He went to bear law school.
Mrs. Smith was clever.
She was no bear's fool.

As intelligent as was this family of bears,
They would soon be thrown
into the midst of
despair.
For something
was lurking
deep in the wood.
Something that
couldn't be seen
 from wherever you
stood.

It wasn't very new,
but very, very old
So old in fact its
origins can't be
told.
This thing I speak
of is called—

BLACK MOLD.

You can't really see it,
until it's too late.
And it waits for no one.
No one—not even fate.

But the bears didn't see it.
So they weren't opposed.
'Til the youngest bear, Darla's,
throat started to close.

The family was frantic
and searching for an antidote,
but nothing could stop the
clog in that little bear's throat.

Darla passed away calmly,
without even a tear.
The rest of the family was
crippled with fear.

"What could have done this?"
"Who? How?"
They were sad, for their daughter's life
was all over now.

They didn't know what to do
So, they called the doctor bear in.
That's when their troubles
began to begin.

The doc found the mold:
In the tiles on the floor
In the roof and the ceiling
and

In hinges of doors
In the sink and garage
In the blender and car
Even in the Smith's brand-new, granite
breakfast bar.
In the carpet and hallways—
it was growing in bounds.

The good doctor said, "Burn the whole
mother down!"

The bears agreed in an instant
and ran for some fire
They lit the place up
and the smoke rose higher.
Higher and higher,
as the Smith's hung their heads.
They were now very homeless
and their only daughter very dead.

If anything comes of this Forest of Damp and
Depression,
It should be that you learned
a very good lesson.
Leave open your windows and
let the sunshine in
Turn on a dehumidifier,
 it isn't a sin.
Quickly clean up spills and
check creases and folds
Or you too may die of the
scourge—

BLACK MOLD.

A moment of solitude

BACKLASH

Performed by Portz & King

Partial monologue transcribed from
unauthorized audio recording

July 4th, New York City

**Music cue: (Ashley only)
Horrible crashing and scales on the
piano**

GREGORY VON PORTZ:

A giant wave came upon us, Goggles
squealed.

And then---------------------------

Recording ends.

*(accidentally erased while trying to
record the sound of
silence in the desert)*

Backlash Promotional Art by Graham McCarty

BACKLASH set list
(In order of appearance)

"Woman of the Ghetto"
"Gloria"
"Family Affair"
"Sweet Dreams"
"Turn the Beat Around"
"Farm House"
"Love Lift Us Up (Where We Belong)"
"I Want It That Way"
"Pumped Up Kicks"
"Walk Like an Egyptian"
"Midnight at the Oasis"
"Egyptian Shumba"
"The Border Song"
"Seven Nation Army"

COUNTY FAIR SING OFF

HOLLYWOOD TWINS:
"If I Die Young"
"Crazy"
"I Hope You Dance"
"Before He Cheats"
"You're Still the One"
"Fancy"
"Love Lift Us Up (Where We Belong)"

PORTZ & KING
"Ashley's Got a Gun"
"Ironic"
"Let Me Blow Your Mind"
"mmmBop"
"Janie's Got a Gun"
"Scream"
"I Try"

FINALE & ASCENSION

"I Wish I Knew How it Would Feel to Be Free"

Item #400

Performing *BACKLASH*

"Euphoria is overrated."

Trite Love Song #2

Portz & King, 2004

Female

My lover's eyes aren't blue like the sky
We don't look in love
to the people passing by
Now I don't care for status and I don't care
for class
But he ain't got no rhythm
And he don't have an ass

Male

She is my princess from a Grimm fairytale
Cause her nose is big and her skin is pale
Her teeth aren't too crooked
And she has a nice smile
But she uses bad grammar

Female

Babe, that's my style

M: When she dances, she moves like a brick
F: And the way he romances
could make anyone sick

Both

I don't like you
I've lately felt
I've hated you all along
But now we're alone and we're singing
this trite love song

F: You make lots of money

M: And you're a good cook

B: I can almost forget
The way that you look

M: Remember those meetings
The ones for my job

F: Oh, I know you've been cheating
I've been sleeping with Bob

F: Whenever you come home,
you always have work

M: Whenever I am naked
all that you do is smirk

<u>Both:</u>
I don't like you
I've lately felt
I've hated you all along
But now we're alone
And we're singing this trite love song

(Sung Simultaneously)

Female:	Male:
You're such a bad dresser	You smell awful
And I can't stand your dog	I hate your perfume
I don't like your music	You burn my waffles
And your haircut is wrong	You're "not in the mood"
I've hated your mother	You take all my money
Since the day that we met	And you spend it on junk
You forget anniversaries	I don't like you honey
And you smoke cigarettes	I should throw you in the trunk

M: You broke my heart

F: Baby, that's how it is

<u>Both:</u>
But we could never part
because of tax purposes

I don't like you
I've lately felt
I've hated you all along

But now that I have taken time,
I feel that I was wrong
Cause you're the best that I can get,
Let bygones be bygones
Cause now we're alone
and we're singing
this trite love song

A Pig, a Lamb and a Wolf
Excerpt from Ashley's Diary
March 17th

"You can't always get what you want," said the pig to the lamb. They were standing outside the gate to animal heaven, which was different than people heaven. In animal heaven, when you walked through the door you emerged on the other side a different creature, ready for another go on God's Green Earth. It reminded the pig of a meat-processing plant. The pig had met his end in a similar plant where he became delicious bacon, but the lamb had never seen one. She had been, primarily, a wool lamb and was eaten by a wolf. Ironically, that very wolf was now standing in line behind them, having been promptly slaughtered by the lamb's shepherd. He seemed to be in shock.

The pig and the lamb were debating their upcoming transformation and their part in it. "I think I would like to be a bug," said the lamb, "because they are not usually eaten by wolves. I would like to avoid that this time, if at all possible. It's not very pleasant."

"Well, I can't say being a bug is much better," replied the pig. "Do you remember what you were in your past life? Before you were a lamb?"

"No. I'm not sure I was anything."

The pig flicked his tail. "I was a fish."

"Oh," said the lamb. "How was that?"

"It was very wet. And dark. I didn't think very much. I kept getting myself confused with all my brothers. Kind of purposeless, really, until a fisherman caught me. I imagine being a bug is a bit like that."

"Hmmm," said the lamb. It was something to think about. They were almost to the front of the line now, and the lamb was getting excited. "Perhaps they will let us walk through together. Then we can be in the same litter! Maybe we will even be wolves! Then nothing can harm us."

"Except for shepherds," chuckled the pig.

Behind them, the wolf whimpered and pawed at his ear. The lamb almost felt sorry for him, but then she remembered the force of his teeth upon her neck.

"Well, whatever we are, I hope we're good," said the lamb.

They were at the front of the line now, the next to go in. Then the door opened and light spilled out all around them.

"See you on the other side," said the lamb, taking a step forward.

"Unless you're a mole," said the pig.

"What's a mole," asked the lamb, but she couldn't hear the answer.

Epilogue

A penguin and a caterpillar stood inside the gate to heaven, waiting to board the ark back to Earth.

The penguin turned to the caterpillar and said "I'm sorry you turned into a bug. I know it's not what you wanted."

"I'm actually fine with it," replied the caterpillar. "I've often wondered what it's like to transform when you know what you'll transform into."

"I'm pleased, too," said the penguin. I've always admired birds, albeit ones that could fly. And I don't believe there are wolves where I'm going, which is nice. "From the Bay of Clouds, a horn sounded.

"Shall we get on board?"

"No," said the Caterpillar. "We still have some time. Let's sit here for a bit and see what the wolf becomes."

They waited quietly for several minutes and watched animals of all kinds emerge in their new forms. Silently, they examined their newly acquired feathers and fur, and then slowly made their way downhill to begin their journey anew. The penguin and the caterpillar saw many fine creatures that day, but eventually turned away, disappointed. The wolf never did appear, for he had become a man.

Excerpt from an untitled police procedural treatment

by Gregory von Portz
copied from page 42

<u>Man Overheard in a Burger King</u>

(*phone rings, he picks up*)

Yeah. Are you comin' over here? Yeah. There are these white punks at the front. I'mma crack they skulls. I'mma go over there and fuck shit up. I'm about to.

Yeah? You gotta help me. I'll be putting a bullet in their skulls. I'll take my gun out and shoot them.

Ok.

See you then.

View from window – Hotel del Mar, Mexico

"Shawl on my Wall"

Unrecorded Song
Portz & King, 2005
(based on a poem by GVP)

There's a Shawl on my Wall
There's a mic stand in the corner
There's a vortex on the floor
And I see the light of the mornin'
is creeping in.

Paint on the windows
Plates on the bed
I go to kiss you
But find out you're dead
You must have died in your sleep

There's a rat on the dresser
Smoking a cigarette
Singing songs about love
Singing songs about messin' around
He says you must have died in your sleep

Portz & King Publicity Photo - never used

You wrote a poem - just like Ashley and
Greg would.

Cruises are slow
You can be close to everyone
Wherever you go.
Cruises are fun;
they take place on the water
To places that are cold & places much hotter.

Greg and Ashley are going on this cruise.
Greg and Ashley like to drink booze.
They'll definitely be doing a show.
Their medleys are quick,
but cruises are slow.

I'm sitting on the same ship.
It's dark in my cabin.
I have a plan,
And wait for it to happen.

A pack of attack dolphins
Swim under the boat.
At my signal they'll knock it
un-afloat.

I'm ready to jump
Jump off the ship.
I hope they survive.
I hope they don't slip.

Once the boat sinks,
Moon Pools will be mine.
They'll sing only for me time, after time, after
time, after time.

Summer Linoleum

from *Inland Seagulls*
a book of short stories
by Gregory von Portz

Between the sound of overweight women doing aerobics to an exercise video and the constant hum of power lines outside, Jeffrey couldn't hear a thing. The electric lines crackled. The screech of his mother and aunts' bare feet doing jumping jacks on linoleum from the downstairs living room echoed up the steps.

Why would they put power lines so close to a window, he thought. He looked at the stains on the carpet. Baby formula stains from years ago. Jeffrey was the kind of boy who would notice things like formula stains on carpets.

His looks were not unlike those of children his age, except for a mole on his back. The mole was nothing special, perhaps a little cancerous, Jeffrey surmised. Nothing that couldn't be removed with a laser. Jeffrey liked the fact that something that was a part of him could be taken so quickly from his body. He saw it once on TV; it excited him.

For an 11 year old, Jeffrey was normal. He rode a bike, and had never been molested by a family member, or anyone! Oh, maybe he was a little chubby, but nothing like his mother, who, at the moment, was swaying from side to side groaning so loudly the air ducts might just burst.

Message in a Wine Bottle VI

Dear Editor,

Like all seasoned song artists, we've experienced performing during our fair share of natural disasters: outdoors, when the pollen count is high, or when a group of dogs all gave birth at the animal shelter we were performing in, but especially during hurricanes. You see, singing at resorts in tropical locations, as we are wont to do, can  be utterly hazardous. And then, the thought of suicide is always lurking beneath the crystal-blue, warm waters, but I digress.

On top of the deadly snakes and bugs, and the latent alcoholism you have to fight on a daily basis, there is— Mother Nature.

We were performing on an island somewhere in Micronesia. It was terrific. The weather was gorgeous. The cannibals had gone organic, so they wanted nothing to do with us. We were doing our act in a little rundown resort called the Hotel del Kai.

The sun, the sea and, oh, that salty air. It's where I discovered I was a bit of a sun worshipper, and Ashley discovered cocaine. I'd walk the beach and comb for treasure. I loved these bluish, volcanic, glassy rocks. They were so beautiful and pure. Like anything I love—I sold them on the internet. I had a little side business called Moon(Pools) Stones. I was raking in the big bucks on that island. (Or clams. LOL. Get it?)

Well, the LOLs stopped as the weather turned. The wind blew and rattled the rafters of the villa I purchased with earnings from Moon(Pools) Stones. Skies darkened. Ashley was on a binge and dancing around the house, "figure skating" with her socks on the slick tile. The rain started.

"Look at me, Greg! I'm Oksana Baiul." Ashley screeched as she did a double axle.

"Ashley, you are going to hurt yourself!" I said.

She didn't listen. I was getting nervous due to the impending storm. My mouth became dry and my breath was awful. I needed a mint. I went through Ashley's purse and got one of those breath strips—the kind that melt in your mouth. The strip melted on my tongue like manna from heaven. It didn't taste like a breath strip. It tasted acidic. Like acid.

The rain became stronger. Strangely, I could feel the rain hit my brain. Each drop a piercing, stabbing knife into the pink folds of my cerebrum.

Drop.
Stab.
Drop.
Stabbing pain.

Now I was really scared for the storm. When would it stop? Would I drown?

"Watch me do a backflip, Greg!" Ashley flipped in the air. She froze for five seconds, it was truly amazing. Then, she fell to the ground directly on her head. Blood poured out of her nose. I couldn't move. The drops were louder than the rain.

Drop.
Stab.
Drop.
Stab. Stab. Stab. Stab. Stab. Pain. Stab. Piercing. Stab. Drop.
My ears! Stab. My eardrums are screaming in agony. Stab. Pain. Drop. Drop. Drop. Pain. Drop. Voices. Shhhh. Stab. Pain. Shhh. I hear voices.

.

From her blood came forth two beings—gods of the island.

"We've seen you steal from our beaches, Gregory. Now we are ready to steal your life from you."

I could taste the rain in my mouth; it tasted like cotton, denim and champagne. Lightning started flashing neon hues of yellow, green and blue. I could see my heart in my ribcage pumping gasoline through my body.

"We need you to give us something—sacrifice something to our volcano god and we will spare you."

I looked around: not my TV, not my new sofa, not my...
Oh my God—I could sacrifice Ashley.

"Why are you picking me up, Greg? I'm a figure skater."

Ashley continued to bitch, as I climbed the volcano in the rain, and, what I now realize to be, tripping on acid from Ashley's purse. I stood at the rim. I took a deep breath. I couldn't do it. I couldn't throw my phone—sorry, Ashley—down into a volcano.

But I did.

The rain stopped.

How to Host Your Own Moon Pools-style Party During a Disaster

Identify your potential disaster
Buy decorations for potential disaster.
For example: mini sandbags for floods
Buy Drinks
Enjoy

Kindness is Edgy,
Gregory von Portz

Ashley's Recipe for Disaster: Emergency Hummus

Ingredients:

A can of beans, any kind, preferably black bean, white bean or chick peas

A couple globs of olive oil

A scoop of tahini or creamy peanut butter

pinch of salt

squeeze of fresh lemon juice (if available)

Instructions:

Use a food processor to combine all ingredients until smooth, waiting to drizzle the olive oil in last. Alternatively, if the power is still out, you can mash everything together with your fists.

Additional flavors can be added, including roasted garlic or hot sauce, which keeps forever. Hummus is an excellent disaster snack as canned beans are typically easy to find, a great source of protein and make other edible things lying around palatable.

Greg's Bonus Disaster Recipe

Water

"Mama, Don't Preach"
Concept for a Jukebox Musical
Assembled by Portz & King
1st public performance -
Moon Pools: Trade Winds

Harlem.

New York City is in the midst of a five-year drought. Many left the city for more moist pastures.

The trees in Central Park are dead.

Christa sits in her childhood room listening to an old record player. Aretha Franklin's "Natural Woman" is playing. The record skips and crackles. Christa sings along.

Songs in Mama, Don't Preach

"Natural Woman"   "Wilderness"
"Livin' on a Prayer"   "My Boo"
"F@&* the Pain Away"   "Stay"
"Fly Me to the Moon"   "Black Water"
"I Don't Mind"   "Kentucky Rain"
"Family Affair"
"Midnight at the Oasis"

Locations:
Christa's Room, Harlem
Jug-a-lugs, a strip club
A Rooftop Oasis
Jerome's Room
A Flood
Mississippi Delta

Item #412

The Harlem Moon

Mama, Don't Preach

A Jukebox Musical by Portz & King

MAMA

You really are something else,
Ms. Christa.

Coming back here after you were
        told not to.

Just who do you think you are?
That's right—

Nobody.

And I, for one, will not have a
        nobody living under my roof.

You keep sayin'…
keep tellin' everyone you're a
        singer.
Then why don't you sing?

Truly, I have never seen somebody
        care less to not sing.

Never.

Don't go giving me the dog eyes
    now, Christa.

You need to leave and find
    yourself.

Lord knows the only thing you're
    finding here is a different
    man in your bed every night.

Don't "But, mom!" me
I know the deal.

What smells like olives?

You ain't singin,
that ain't bringing no money in.

Sticky (I'm So Hot)

by Gregory von Portz

I'm so hot,
Like performance fleece
You wanna rent me?
I'll break the lease

I don't sit down,
I rise like yeast.

When the bread's all done
We gonna have a feast.

And dance
Gitchy to Gitchy
Ya to Ya-Da
Gimme some money,
And you get the dada

We rock this party
From block to block

Make you sweat so hard
You gotta change your socks
We go up and down
Like the NASDAQ stock
Exchange our numbers
And put this thing on lock.

They call me Evian
'Cause I flow like water
If I was on fire,
I wouldn't be hotter
When my choocie's on,
You better hide your daughters

Now that's E to the V
V to the ON
Getting kinky in your Bed,
Bath & Beyond
If I was seventeen,
I'd take you to the prom.
Get you pregnant,
Name the baby Salon.
Prom Baby

Pigeon of the Seas Cruise Ship Cabaret Performer Contract

This agreement is made between Pigeon of the Seas Cruise Line (hereinafter referred to as the "Presenter") and Gregory von Portz and Ashley Rebecca King (aka Moon Pools), if more than one, listed on Addendum A attached hereto and included herein (hereinafter referred to as the "Artist"), by and through their designated agent or representative ("Manager") identified below.

WHEREAS, Presenter conducts the event known as: Around the World in 560 Days Cruise by Pigeon of the Seas (hereinafter referred to as the "Performance "); and von Portz and King

WHEREAS, Presenter desires to hire Artist, as independent contractor(s), to provide the Performance generally described below (the "Performance").

WHEREAS, Artist(s) desire to provide such Performance;

The parties agree as follows:

1. Artists: The names and addresses of the Artist who will appear during the Performance, the amounts to be paid to each.

2. Agent/Manager: The name and mailing address of the Representative, who is executing this Agreement on behalf of Artist(s), is: Elizabeth "Betty" "Z" Ralston.

3. Place of Performance: The place of performance is at

The ocean on a cruise ship.

4. Date(s) and Time(s) of Performance:

The date(s) of the Performance shall be immediate and the time(s) of the Performance shall be 1pm, 2pm, 3am, 6am. This Performance shall be 1 hour(s) with no intermission.

5. Performance: The Performance is generally described as: A cover band, a karaoke performance, menacing, akin to rape. But what it really is, is a show about kindness and sharing and caring.

6. Agreement to Perform: Artist(s) agree to provide the Performance in accordance with the terms of this Agreement and any addendums or riders hereto.

7. Price of Performance: Presenter agrees to pay Artist or his agent an aggregate of Six-hundred thousand DOLLARS ($600,000) for the Performance by cheque immediately

following the Performance. The cheque shall be made payable to: Gregory von Portz. (Ashley Rebecca King is not to be trusted with checks, as she collects paper and will never cash it.)

8. Recording, Reproduction or Transmission of Performance: Presenter will use its best efforts to prevent the recording, reproduction or transmission of the Performance without the written permission of Artist(s) or Artist's representative.

9. Excuse of Obligations: Presenter and Artist shall be excused from their obligations hereunder in the event of proven sickness, accident, riot, strike, epidemic, except for the sinking of the ship and animal uprisings.

In Witness Hereof, this Agreement is executed on the date first above written.

Presenter (Authorized signature)

By: Mr. Pigeon

Artist/Agent or Manager representative

By: *Gregory von Portz & Ashley Rebecca King*

Post-Show Street Fair- New York City, NY

Portz & King at home

Possible Portz & King sighting(?)

Haiku
Excerpt from Ashley's Diary
September 8th

On a one-sailed boat

4 hands, 2 heads and a bird

We aim to please you.

Message in a Wine Bottle VII

(Possibly written prior to message VI,
but obtained at a later date)

Dear Editor,

If a tree falls in the woods, and falls on someone, and they die instantly, and no one is around until long after the body starts decomposing—is the tree a murderer?

Ashley and I were faced with this question while performing in the Redwood Forest in California. We had been asked to perform at the memorial service of our dear friend Olivia from Malibu. She died as she lived, with hate in her heart, booze in her blood and an ax in her hand. 'Liv was going through a very messy divorce, and just lost the house in Malibu. We all felt terrible for her. She decided to go on a hike in the Redwood National Forest, her favorite place because she loved moss. All she wanted to do was eat her low-carbohydrate snacks amid the moss.

It was all fun and games, until a tree fell on her, and killed her.

Enter Moon Pools with our funeral set.

We held a memorial for her in the woods, where she died. Our set opened with "Love Machine" and ended with "End of the Road."

During the voodoo ritual portion, Ashley kicked over all of the candles, and we stood there as the whole forest was engulfed in flames. People always say that natural light is best, but you don't really know it until you see the pictures.

RIP, Olivia!

Kindness is Edgy,
Gregory von Portz

"Señor Muerte"

Portz & King, 2004

Señor Muerte
Rides in from the South
With a Sombrero
And a cigar in his mouth
His eyes are blue
But his heart, his heart is black
He'll steal your lover in the night
And never give her back
Señor Muerte

It was a Sunday
When I heard the cursed doorbell
And my love answered
To a python straight from hell
Señor Muerte
His heart, his heart is black
He took my lover on that night
He'll never give her back

With blood stains on his shirt
You may think that he's a slobbo
But I know,
I know he is
El Diablo

Instrumental/ Spoken dialogue (Spanish)

When you wake up you may find there's
nothing left
Because Señor Muerte
(*Spoken*) To you
Means "Mister Death"

Moon Pools: So Emotional

A tribute to the death of Whitney Houston

Opening - Jazz Funeral
 "How Will I Know?"
 "Going Up Yonder"

GREGORY VON PORTZ:

Ladies and Gentlemen, we are here to celebrate something very special - the untimely passing of our dear friend, Midgy Bonilla . Her favorite artist was not Whitney Houston, but we always thought she should be.

 "I' m Your Baby Tonight"
 "Where Do Broken Hearts Go?"
 "One of Those Days"
 "I Get So Emotional"
 "Heartbreak Hotel"
 "Exhale (Shoop)"
 "My Name is Not Susan"
 "Million Dollar Bill"
                (Collect $ from fans)
 "I' m Every Woman*"*
                (Dance- off)
 "I Have Nothing"

"Step by Step"

"Greatest Love of All" /
               "One Moment in Time"

Intermission – "Star Spangled Banner"

"Queen of the Night"

"It' s Not Right, but It' s Okay"
              (Show Greg the receipts)

A Medley for All the Lovers
"You Give Good Love"
"Saving All My Love for You"
"All the Man That I Need"

"We Got Something in Common"
         (We welcome our special guest)

Final Medley
"I Will Always Love You
"My Love is Your Love"
"Count on Me"
"I Didn' t Know My Own Strength"
"Didn' t We Almost Have it All?"
"Run to You"
"When you Believe"
"I Believe in You and Me"
"I Wanna Dance with Somebody"
Ending: "I Will Always Love You"
"I Try"

Item #212: Greg's set list

Message in a Wine Bottle VIII

Are you getting these letters? Stop working on our book, and call the fucking police. Ashley and I received an invitation to do a show on the island. We are the only people on the island!

We went to sleep last night, drunk on some fermented coconut water (my recipe), and woke up. Cheryl, I kid you not--there is now a recreation of the Hotel del Mar, the original one Ashley and I used to perform in years ago. I don't know how it happened. I'm not dreaming this. Ashley says it's real, too. Is this mass hysteria?

Here's what the "invite" says:

Dear Gregory and Ashley,

You are required to perform, poolside, under the moon. I'll see you tonight.

I am terrified.

Kindness is edgy,
Gregory von Portz

Hey, you. Yeah...you.

Hear them bottles a'clanking? Yep, you do.

Every one of those bottles Greg sent out, you have. You put them into a book—this book.

Stop laughing. **Now.**

Cabaret Favorites Assumed Dead after "Death Boat" cruise company Ship Capsizes

by Deborah Grace Ann
Additional reporting by Big Greg Smith

New York, NY- Cabaret "song artists" Gregory von Portz and Ashley Rebecca King, also known as Moon Pools, were involved in the bizarre sinking of the *Pigeon of the Sea* cruise ship the S.S. Janelle. Three weeks ago, the vessel was capsized by a pack of dolphins. The dolphins are believed to have been former Yugoslavian attack animals. All passengers aboard are accounted for except for three people including Von Portz and King. The third missing person is believed to have boarded the ship under a pseudonym. *Pigeon of the Sea* is known for having lax security and is the subject of an ongoing investigation by Homeland Security.

Pigeon of the Sea has been involved in a number of accidents in the past two months including the suicide of everyone on a ship. Police say the conditions on the ships were so terrible, and the towels so rough that all 400, including the captain, decided to jump.

We contacted the president of *Pigeon of the Sea* and he said. "Hello. I told you not to call me at work, my wife tracks the calls." When

216

asked for a comment he said. "So sorry. I no speak English. English no good for me. Is not my first, how you say, language."

Officials are not hopeful of a live recovery for the most recent tragedy. "The ocean is real big," said one searcher.

The pair's agent, Elizabeth Ralston, had this to say when contacted for a comment, "Oh. They were in an accident?" She is, however, hopeful for their safe return. "Those idiots are the only income I have right now. They better have the legs and the arms of a manatee. I can't believe this. I'm just processing this at the moment: I'm really screwed. God damn it. I have to go."

Ralston added that she was going to set up a memorial fund which would benefit her.

Item #711

Sake Maker

from *Inland Seagulls*
a book of short stories
by Gregory von Portz

I cannot calculate the amount of time I've been here into Western years. My jaw sometimes hurts from the rice, but I do not mind it. This is my purpose. This is where I belong. Home is on an island, in the southern part of the country. My father was a fisherman. My mother was a mother to three sisters and I.

Chewing becomes easy for the body to remember. You put rice in mouth, chew, then spit it into a pot made from clay. Thick, heavy clay. Heavy as my heart was when the boat took us here. We weren't prisoners, but it felt like that.

"Happiness must hurt," my mother used to always say. Happiness is a sharp pain in the top of your chest. Happiness is my memories of fish on a line gasping for water.

I chew. And spit.

My mother always told me that spitting was for lower-class people, like Midori who lived down the street. She smoked cigarettes and spit. She was not taken away on the boat. She was not a virgin. The clay pot fills with my saliva and rice polished by my teeth. Outsiders find the brown gruel repulsive, as I did at first. Now, I find comfort in the mash. I have good teeth.

That is why they chose me. Midori has bad teeth.

I rapaciously gnaw on fistful after fistful of rice. Sometimes a rice grain makes its way down my throat, and I gag. I cannot vomit though, that would ruin all of the hard work. I must not be the one to ruin the sake. After I chew and spit, and all of the other women here do, they will leave the pots out to collect spirits from the air. The spirits have magical powers, I have heard. They will change this mixture into alcohol.

My father was drinking sake on the morning I left. He did not drink very much. Father said it was to celebrate the good news of my position with the sake company. I knew it would be a very long time before I'd see him.

Dozens of girls are sitting next to me in the chewing room. Fist-chew-spit. After shifts, we talk about boys back home, and compare our teeth. My teeth are always the whitest. My mother said that is because I could not drink tea when I was younger. The rest of the girls have tea-stained teeth. And it is very much a shame, because many are pretty otherwise.

My only friend here is Michi. She is my friend because we both experienced the death of a loved one at the same age: twenty-five. That was when our paternal grandmothers died, separately, of course, and in different years, since she is five years older than me. But I find it odd that we both experienced the death of a loved one at the same age. We were too old. Michi does not have good teeth. She eats candy, which we are not supposed to do. The sugar will ruin the sake.

A grain runs down my throat and hits both sides like a ping-pong ball. I hold in a sneeze. The security guard eyes me. I may not sneeze, for it will ruin the sake. I know what will happen if I ruin the sake. I hold my sneeze in. I pray to my ancestors that I do not sneeze. I spit the rice out quickly and take a deep breath. My bucket is almost full and my jaw is almost stiff. Michi smiles at me, and wipes the back of her hand across her forehead in relief.

I sneeze.

Walking in the shadows of gods

Excerpt from Ashley's Diary
March 27th

Flying isn't so hard
You must only lift your feet from the ground
both at once
and transform.
It takes breath support
and faith
and courage
but it can be done
Once I could not crawl
then I could not walk
then I could not run
So tomorrow
I may very well fly

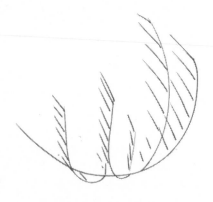

You've done it! You're going to have a personal audience with Moon Pools. Do you think they'll like you? (They had better.) This is the most exciting thing that's ever happened in your life. Your favorite cover band is going to be singing just for you. They never do requests, but you know they'll do it for you, 'cause you gave them a request list. Moon Pools better pay attention to you after all of the attention you paid them.

It's all you. Your wisdom and stupidity got you this. You thank the tiki gods who have been watching over you for some time. You've been watching over Greg and Ashley for some time, too. Even though you've seen all of their shows, you've never met them. They were always "too busy." But out here on this island, they have nothing else to do. You hate them. Hate them for what they've made your life become. You're a Moon Pools addict. It's as addictive as heroin, but takes a harder toll on you than any opiate ever could. You've lost teeth for Moon Pools, you've lost your friends and family. You've even had your dog taken away from you. Tonight you kick this fucking Moon Pools habit for good.

What are you going to wear? Fancy? Casual? You're so excited; it feels like a first date. You hope the hotel you made for them (not without casualties) is sufficient. And the sound system, too. And the lighting. Heart beating—your heart is beating. You hope they like the clothes you bought for them. You even got their favorite fragrances; you are wearing both of them at the same time. It's making you dizzy.

"Five minutes to places." you yell out of your window.

"FIVE MINUTES TO PLACES!"

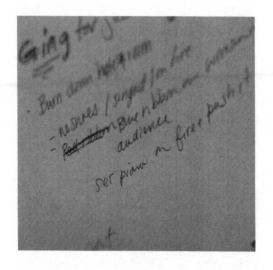

Item #291: Ashley's Notes *(BACKLASH)*

Opening Monologue from
In a Polynesian Mood
Transcribed from bootleg video recording
(song cues omitted)

It's those moments in the night when you're
roused from your sleep and wake up
suddenly, unexpectedly, and you realize that
your most sacred hopes and dreams may not
come true. It's the things you've thought of
that have never left your head, secret dreams
you've only known of. You know, I've heard
that you are only as sick as your secrets and if
that is the case—I'm terminal. Tonight, I
thought I'd share it with you.

I get into these moods. Really deep,
thoughtful depressions that take a long time
to shake. Sometimes, they manifest
themselves in horrible ways: I'll stop talking,
stop eating, stop laughing. But then I realize
that someone, somewhere on this wide
expanse of humanity, is having an unwanted
pregnancy. That makes me feel so much
better.

I like driving. It really calms me down.

I remember driving on summer nights, those
that made you resentful of the present,
because all you could think about was the
future.

Beautiful fever dreams of who you would
become, the places you would go.

A pink moon on the rise and fireflies.

I used to drive through thunderstorms in an
old Chrystler LeBarron convertible with the
top down, and cover the seats with garbage
bags and towels. You could feel everything on
those drives—the rain, the wind, the static
electricity in the air crackling down winding
country roads in the summer.

I'd listen to 89.9 Temple Public Radio,
broadcasting from Philadelphia, PA. Nina
Simone, Anita O'day, Sarah Vaughn and
sometimes music live from the Zanzibar Blue
on 200 South Broad Street.

Everything was so new.

I could have been anything or anyone.

I really wanted to sing jazz. 89.9 would be
bringing you my listener-supported radio
special commercial free. Gregory von Portz
LIVE from the Zanzibar Blue. I would have
sung my set to the sounds of glasses and
plates clanking on tables, giving my ethereal
performance some grounding in
reality. Then, I'd probably move to Los
Angeles, and have a weekly residency at the
Troubadour. Every other month or so, I'd jet
to the east coast to do a night or two at the

Blue Note or The Village Underground or Birdland or-or-or-or...there were so many options for me.

Instead, here I am with Ashley Rebecca King, in this dump. It's not that I don't love it here, but even with the beautiful curtains, it is like my grandmother says: "You can't shine shit."

Yes, Ashley and I have been working together for a long time. Pre 9/11, even. You see, Ashley had dreams of become a performer, too. She wanted to be a dancer—not just any dancer—the best tapper this side of the Mason-Dixon line. Ashley was always tapping: tap, tap, tap. And from the reviews I've read in the Sewickly Herald Star—she was actually quite talented. But like so many dancers, she suffered the fate of becoming a yoga instructor.

Zanzibar Blue

The air in the room had that combination of nervous excitement and dread that only first-time mothers experience: how the fuck will this turn out?

Gregory von Portz and Ashley Rebecca King are on a stage, on an island, in a hotel. Are they the victims of circumstance? Or do they deserve this? There's smoke in the air. The lone person in the audience is slowly smoking. Through the spotlights, all Greg and Ashley see is a shadow and occasionally the neon, sun-colored ember of this person taking a drag.

Greg's mouth is dry and hot. He doesn't know if he'll be able to sing. He and Ashley have an escape planned. They drew it out in the sand last night, and then erased it after they memorized it. Early escapes had been met by the clicking squeals of the attack dolphins surrounding the island. Ashley's hands tremble.

The person smoking thought these two might come up with some sort of escape plan. So the shadowy figure has their own.

Music from the piano fills the air, jarring—jarring nuts and bolts being dropped into a metal bucket. The three people in that small recreation of a hotel club are covered in sweat. Not from the heat, from the nerves.

Greg brings the mic to his mouth. He reaches over, and grabs the sole audience member's hand...

"Ladies and gentlemen....

welcome to Moon Pools."

Bossa Nova Tiki

by Gregory von Portz

They revisited the river—the pond.

There's a certain sound

and the novice draws the blind

The world is round

but I don't know

I don't know

The joker's laugh

And my flower says:

Ah, Tiki.

How the bends of your arms

make me love you, Tiki

All of you,Tiki

Beautiful, Tiki

Tiki

There is just one voice that's important

I fly with you, Tiki

I feel you, Tiki.

All of you, Tiki.

Beautiful, Tiki.

If you knew the one voice that you love was
important.
Fickle, Tiki.
Hear it, Tiki.

The waters run now with the pain of years.
But my life is hope in you.

Speak now, Tiki.
This is how it should be always, Tiki.
I adore you, Tiki.
How I adore you.

There are so many beautiful things to see.
That we both can see, Tiki.

Portz & King (not in that order)

Everyone likes to think their life will be meaningful and important. For the most part, that never happens. Luckily for us, our lives have meaning.

How do we do it? That's easy: discipline and hydration.

Tips for living the Moon Pools Lifestyle:

-Be disciplined.

-Drink purified water.

-Take long walks.

-Perform often, in big city venues.

-Have people review your show for major publications.

-Love

-Never underestimate the importance of lemons.

-Take Revenge.

-Consume Ten cups of green tea per day.

-Limit meat to chicken, pork, beef and rabbit.

-Love yourself.

-Take long, hot baths, until skin prunes. Then jump out of the shower and rub Vaseline all over your body.

-Hire a masseuse.

-Always Remember: *Kindness is Edgy*.

237

MOON POOLS: KINDESS IS EDGY

The Collection

Additional Items:

ASHLEY'S DIARY

BACKLASH

DOGS DON'T LOVE, THEY DIE

INLAND SEAGULLS

MESSAGE IN A WINE BOTTLE

RECIPES

ORIGINAL SONGS

TRAVELOGUES

PHOTO CREDITS

Page # 16   Graham McCarty

Page # 19   Adam King

Page # 42   GVP

Page # 55   GVP

Page # 62   ARK

Page # 71   GVP

Page # 88   GVP

Page # 94   GVP

Page # 109   GVP

Page # 113   GVP

Page # 124   GVP

Page # 129   GVP

Page # 131   GVP

Page # 133   Graham McCarty

Page # 143 (1)   Graham McCarty

Page # 143 (2)   Elizabeth Ralston

Page # 143 (3)   Allyson King

Page # 158   GVP

Special Thanks to our editor – Cheryl BreaKing

This book goes out to anyone who's ever died from having too much of a good time!

It's also a tribute to our fans, or Pool Boys and Pool Girls, as they're called.

We'd like to thank them for supporting us:

David Beck

Kerry Blaum

Eleanor Brea

Melissa Cabe

Meagan, Dennis, Ava & Kate Cornelius

J.W. Crump

Jonathan Desley

Danielia Donohue Reidy

William Dooner

Irene Dotter

Alex Farlow

Alyssa Farlow

Matt Fornataro

Heather Frye

Julie Galorenzo

Stacey Hartsell Rywelski

Nancy Hester

Stacey Higgins

Carol Hill

Sherry Houston

Hilary Kennedy

Rosey Kerestus Stianche

Adam King

Allyson King

Richard & Cheryl King

Craig & Judy King

Lindsay Levesque

Kara Levy

Brooke Lewis

Pam Lewis

Marie McAndrew

Dana & Mike McCarty

Graham McCarty

Lauren McDonald

K.K. McDonald

Carla Nagar

Courtney Navitsky

Michael Newman

Sarah Nowak

Melissa O'Donnell

Meighan Pallone

Amanda Peck

Peggy Peck

Karen Petrosky Blaum

Tony & Rachel Phillippe

Chris & Sam Pin

Greg & Deborah Portz

Alec Portz

Elizabeth Ralston

Jennifer Riegle

Erica Ryan

Cynthia & John Toth

Andrew Walter

Colin Ward

Corey Ward

Marsha Wheat

Ashley Rebecca King is a daughter, sister and wife. More importantly, she is an actor, writer and performer. Her main goal in life is to "get attention and I don't care how" and play with cats. Born in Pittsburgh to educators, Ashley fell in love with the arts at a young age. Theater and movies let her imagine a world outside of her bedroom, which was good since she was a loner and rarely left. King has enjoyed success on stages in NYC and around the country.

Gregory von Portz is a writer, performer and international personality. He's called himself "a veritable mixture of French luxury, intercontinental exoticism, and authentic American consumerism." His sainted parents and brother endured his endless terrible piano playing and dramatic antics, so after an almost two-decade stint in small-town Pennsylvania, he moved to New York City where he likes to walk—a lot.

Portz & King

Portz & King have been working together far longer than they'd like to admit. After meeting on the steps of a midtown bar, they began performing at Danny's Skylight Room where they would go on after Blossom Dearie. (Only later would they realize how cool that actually was.)

Together they've created dozens of original shows from basement-cabarets to fully-realized theatrical productions. They've even written a book—the one you just read.
They both have very different tastes in music.

The preceding biographies are dedicated to Blossom Dearie.

22109148R00152

Made in the USA
Middletown, DE
21 July 2015